Northumberland & Tyneside

A Miscellany

Glen Lyndon Dodds

Albion
Press

Albion Press
40 Park Parade Roker Sunderland Tyne & Wear
ISBN 978 0 9525122 9 5

For more information on Albion Press titles
email albionpress@gmail.com

Cover photographs: The Tyne bridges at Newcastle and Hexham Abbey
Back cover photograph: Bamburgh Castle

Typeset and designed by UpStyle Book Design
www.upstyledesign.co.uk

Printed and bound in Great Britain by
Berforts Information Press Ltd
23-25 Gunnels Wood Park, Gunnels Wood Road
Stevenage, Hertfordshire SG1 2BH

CONTENTS

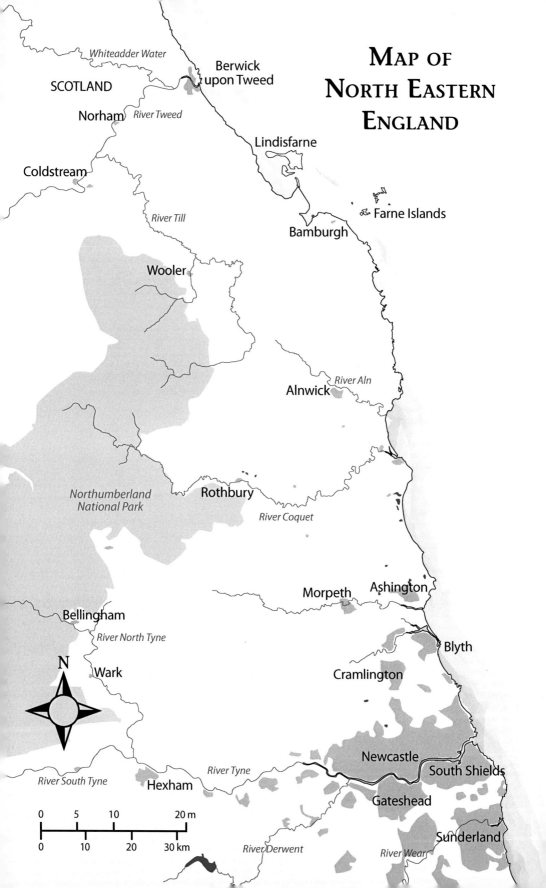

PREFACE

This book touches on aspects of the history of places for which I have a great deal of affection. Northumberland is certainly one of my favourite counties, a place where I have enjoyed numerous day trips and several holidays and whose landscapes and heritage have an enduring appeal. I am also very fond of Tyneside, which although undoubtedly less scenic nevertheless contains much of interest.

Most of the text is new but some of the chapters originally appeared in *The Northumbrian*, an excellent magazine whose first issue was published in 1987, and for which I have had the pleasure of writing a number of articles since 1999.

I wish to thank Kathy Smith of the Morpeth Music Society for providing me with information and photographs, and Elaine Bowden of the Alnwick and District Choral Society for her equally enthusiastic assistance. I also want to thank Peter Ayres, Darren Turner and Richard Billen for generously providing photographs.

Glen Lyndon Dodds,
Sunderland, 19 May 2013

ALNWICK,
NORTHUMBERLAND'S DUCAL TOWN

Alnwick stands on elevated ground on the south side of the little River Aln, and is a fascinating town whose most famous building, Alnwick Castle, houses one of the finest private art collections in Britain.

The origins of Alnwick (whose name means 'farm by the Aln') are unclear, but the settlement was granted the status of a borough by William de Vescy, the baron of Alnwick, during the second half of the 12th century and was centred on a triangular marketplace. One of the highways that converged on the market was the Great North Road, the main route from Newcastle to Berwick upon Tweed, and as a result the town witnessed much coming and going.

After 1420, parliamentary elections for Northumberland were held in Alnwick, and this brought members of the county's gentry to the town to participate in the elections. Moreover, in 1433 the borough received permission to erect a town wall and in the years that followed substantial defences were provided and included the Hotspur Gate, which still survives at the southeast end of the historic core of the town. The approach to this gateway is known as Bondgate Without—formerly part of the Great North Road—whereas the section of the same street once enclosed by the town defences is called Bondgate Within.

A much larger and more imposing medieval building than the Hotspur Gate, is Alnwick parish church, St Michael's. This lies in the northwest part of the town and was rebuilt in the late 15th century (little earlier fabric was retained) and is Northumberland's finest Perpendicular church.

In the field of education, a grammar school and a song school are known to have existed at Alnwick in the Tudor period for a report of 1549 records the existence of 'Landes and possessions belonging to the use and typend [stipend] of two Preests, the one master of a grammer scoole and thother master of a synge scoole, within Alnewyke afforseyd.'

In subsequent centuries, Alnwick experienced little development until the 18th century. Among buildings erected during that century was the town hall on Fenkle Street: it dates from 1731, is pierced by an arched passageway linking the street to the marketplace (located immediately to the east) and is surmounted by a clock tower built or rebuilt in 1767. It was, however, only as the century drew to a close that the town entered a significant phase of rebuilding and growth. Consequently, in 1822 William Davison observed: 'The town of Alnwick is, on the whole, well built, and the streets are in general judiciously disposed. The houses, being built mostly of freestone, have a noble appearance; and the thatched houses, which are

The Hotspur Gate

numerous in all old towns, are here rapidly disappearing, and giving place to others which approach to elegance.' Davison also states that the weekly market was held on Saturday and was 'a large market for corn and provisions of various kinds, the adjoining country being very fertile. The corn is mostly sold by sample, and is sent principally to London.' He also records that Alnwick enjoyed 'one of the best and cheapest fish-markets in the kingdom. It is held near the front of the Town-hall, and receives a regular and plentiful supply from Newton, Craster, Boulmer, Alemouth [Alnmouth] and the neighbouring fisheries.'

Shortly thereafter, Pigot's *National Commercial Directory* of 1834 stated:

> The streets of Alnwick are, in general, wide and well paved; its shops are numerous and respectable, with several good inns. The town is admirably supplied with water...and it is well lighted with gas.... The trade of the town is [almost] entirely of a local nature.... On the town moor, bricks and tiles are made; and the trade in corn is by no means inconsiderable.

Among other things, the ensuing Victorian era saw the arrival of the railway in 1850—a branch line of the Newcastle and Berwick Railway—and the establishment of the *Alnwick Mercury* in 1854, a paper that is now the *Northumberland Gazette*. Moreover, Hardy's fish-tackle manufacturing business was founded in 1872. The firm still exists and enjoys a worldwide reputation.

St Michael's Church

In addition to branches of national chains such as Boots and W.H. Smith, the town also contains a number of well-established independent stores. A case in point is Jobson's (near the Hotspur Gate), a family-run business that sells outdoor wear and is famous for the quality of its saddlery department. Jobson's has occupied its current premises for around 80 of its 100 years or so of existence. Alnwick is also home to Barter Books, one of the largest secondhand and antiquarian bookshops in Britain. The business dates from 1991, is located in the former Victorian railway station on the southern approach to the Hotspur Gate, and has been described by the *New Statesmen* as 'the British Library of secondhand bookshops.'

Among businesses located on Bondgate Within, is the White Swan Hotel—formerly the town's premier coaching inn. The hotel's remarkable Olympic Suite restaurant has stained-glass windows, wooden panelling, mirrors and other fixtures from *Titanic's* sister ship, RMS *Olympic*.

Entertainment venues include Alnwick Playhouse, located in a former 700-seat cinema that opened on Bondgate Without in 1925; a cinema that sadly closed in 1979 after its fortunes had waned for a number of years. The building subsequently faced demolition, but was saved when it was purchased in 1984 by the Northumberland Theatre Company—now known as the NTC Touring Theatre Company—a small professional touring group that uses the ground floor for rehearsals and administrative purposes. The

The marketplace and town hall

company leases the upper floor to the Alnwick and District Playhouse Trust, which has transformed the derelict balcony into a multi-purpose 262-seat arts venue where audiences enjoy a varied programme of theatrical performances, music and films. The Playhouse was opened in December 1990 by Henry Percy, the 11th Duke of Northumberland, and of this exciting development the *Northumberland Gazette* rightly noted: 'Years of hard work have gone into its refurbishment…[and] the magnificent result is worthy of their efforts and all involved deserve high praise for adding another jewel to Alnwick's crown.'

In short, Alnwick is a desirable place to visit or live. The population numbers around 8,000 and many of the residents commute to work on Tyneside or elsewhere.

The main visitor attractions are the castle and Alnwick Garden. The former began as an earth and timber fortress in the Norman period and was rebuilt in stone during the 12th century. Not surprisingly, it has had a dramatic history. For example, in 1173 and 1174—when the castle was held by the Vescy family—it was unsuccessfully besieged by King William the Lion of Scotland. Moreover, in the early 1460s during the Wars of the Roses, the castle was held in turn by Lancastrian and Yorkist garrisons on more than one occasion. By then, the lords of Alnwick were the Percys,

Opposite: The impressive Grand Cascade

who had become barons of Alnwick in 1309 and were made Earls of North-umberland in 1377.

For various reasons, the Percys neglected the castle during the 16th and 17th centuries and spent most of their time in the South. However, in the mid 18th century a major programme of restoration was carried out by the first Duke and Duchess of Northumberland (the dukedom was bestowed in 1766) and they transformed the castle into their main country seat. Further-more, Algernon, the fourth duke, who held the title in the years 1847-65, enlarged the keep and redecorated the state rooms in a style that reflects his love of Renaissance Italy.

Alnwick Castle is still the home of the Percys and Jane, the wife of the 12th duke (who inherited the title from his brother in 1995), has created the splendid Alnwick Garden which is located nearby and was officially opened in 2002. It was designed by Belgian experts, and the main feature is the Grand Cascade, a 'magnificent tumbling mass of water with spell-binding displays.'

ALNWICK & DISTRICT CHORAL SOCIETY

Over the years, a number of admirable societies dedicated to the performance of classical music have enriched life for the residents of Alnwick and its environs.

For example, a programme survives for the Alnwick Amateur Choral Society's tenth concert. The event, which included music by Handel, was held in the Town Hall on the evening of Tuesday, 1 May 1860. Moreover, in the early 20th century a soprano from South Africa named Ada Forrest, visited Alnwick to perform at a concert given by the Alnwick Choral Union, whose patrons were the seventh Duke and Duchess of Northumberland. The concert was held at the Corn Exchange on Tuesday 12 December 1911, and Miss Forrest (who had recently sung before King George V and Queen Mary at the Royal Albert Hall) performed music by various composers including Schubert.

Later still, in 1933, the Alnwick and District Choral Society was formed. Although its activities were interrupted by the ensuing world war—some members kept choral music alive on a modest level at Alnmouth—the society restarted in earnest in 1947.

A regular programme of concerts has been held by the society in

Heather Burns, Paul Rendall, the dowager Duchess of Northumberland,
Paul Gibson, Claire McKenna and Peter Brown on 27 March 2011

parish churches, halls and at Alnwick Playhouse. For instance, on 22 April 1950, St Paul's Parish Church (a Victorian building designed by Anthony Salvin) was the venue for a performance of Haydn's magnificent oratorio, *The Creation.* Furthermore, on a few occasions the society has performed abroad, as was true in 1999 when it gave concerts in Vienna.

Following the devastating Asian tsunami on Boxing Day 2004, the society held a benefit concert at St Paul's Church on 23 January 2005 and raised £1,030 on behalf of the survivors. More recently still, on 27 March 2011, the same venue was used for a well-received concert whose entire programme was devoted to music by Mozart, most notably his famous *Requiem.* The soloists were Heather Burns, Paul Rendall, Paul Gibson and Claire McKenna. Since 2010, the society's musical director has been Peter Brown, a native of Somerset who won an organ scholarship to Oxford University.

One of the society's stalwarts is Elizabeth, the dowager Duchess of Northumberland, of whom Elaine Bowden comments, 'she has been a most supportive President of the Choral Society since 1947.'

Opposite: The choir, conductor and soloists following a
concert of music by Mozart on 27 March 2011

BAMBURGH,
AN HISTORIC AND ENCHANTING VILLAGE

The historic village of Bamburgh lies on the coast of Northumberland, and is dominated by one of England's most spectacular castles, a former stronghold that stands majestically on a basalt outcrop overlooking the North Sea.

The castle dates from the Norman era, but the site has a much older history. It was probably occupied by an Iron Age fort and was certainly the location of an Anglo-Saxon citadel known as Bebbanburh.

The Germanic presence began in the mid 6th century when an Anglo-Saxon warlord named Ida gained control of Bamburgh and its environs. Ida founded a line of kings, and his successors ruled the vast kingdom of Northumbria, a realm founded in the early 7th century that stretched northward from the Humber into Scotland, and as far west as the Irish Sea.

Bamburgh was one of the most important places in the kingdom and the Northumbrian historian, Bede (c.673-735), tells us that in the mid 7th century it attracted the attention of Penda, an arch-enemy of Northumbria, who marched north with an army from the Midlands. Penda 'reached the very gates of the royal city, which takes its name from Bebba, a former queen' but was not able to capture Bamburgh. Therefore, he pulled down the neighbouring villages and 'carried to Bamburgh a vast quantity of beams, rafters, wattled walls, and thatched roofs, piling it high around the city wall on the landward side' and, when the wind was favourable, 'set fire to this mass.' However, prayers of a saintly figure named Aidan, who was watching events on nearby Farne Island, caused the wind to change direction towards Penda's forces. Therefore, they abandoned the attempt to destroy 'a city so clearly under God's protection.'

The kingdom of Northumbria was later destroyed by the Vikings, and by the early tenth century what is now the county of Northumberland was ruled by a native family based at Bamburgh. This remained the case until the mid 11th century.

After the Norman Conquest, Bamburgh became the property of Robert de Mowbray, the Earl of Northumberland. He rebelled against William II in 1095, whereupon Bamburgh Castle was besieged by the king's troops. Mowbray escaped from the fortress at night and sailed southward, but was nevertheless captured on Tyneside and escorted back to Bamburgh where the castle was held on his behalf by his wife and nephew. Hearing that the earl would be blinded if they did not immediately surrender, they capitulated and Bamburgh became a royal castle and remained so until 1610, by which time it was in a poor state of repair.

Opposite: Bamburgh Castle
viewed from the village

In 1295 the borough of Bamburgh, which lay on lower ground a short distance inland, was one of only three places in Northumberland that sent MPs to parliament. However, as Frederick Bradshaw has commented, in Bamburgh's case this 'was more a compliment to its past glory and the strength of its castle than to its wealth or population.' The borough, centred on the present village green, was certainly modest and outclassed by several other boroughs in Northumberland. It did not send MPs again and ultimately lost its borough status.

Inevitably, the lives of Bamburgh's residents were disrupted by Anglo-Scottish conflict, when the region was often raided by the enemy. It was not just Scots who exploited the situation. In the early 14th century local folk who sought sanctuary in the castle were fleeced by the castellan. He forced them to pay for sheltering in the stronghold, plundered their goods, and made unreasonable financial demands.

During the Wars of the Roses, the castle was besieged on several occasions and was held, in turn, by both contending parties. For example, in March 1463 the castellan, Sir Ralph Percy, swopped sides and so the Lancastrian, Henry VI, proceeded to make Bamburgh his base. Consequently, in early 1464 his supporters conducted various military sorties from the castle. Later that year, though, Henry fled from Northumberland and Yorkist troops moved against Bamburgh. Indeed, the castle was subjected to a battering by royal ordnance and stormed. The commander, Ralph Grey, who had been seriously wounded was duly executed in Yorkshire.

The castle was in ruinous condition when Lord Crewe, the Bishop of Durham, purchased Bamburgh in 1704. The prelate bequeathed the castle

for charitable purposes and, in the 1750s, his trustees began a lengthy programme of restoration. Among other things, the mid-12th century keep was made habitable once more.

In 1894 the historic site was bought by the first Lord Armstrong of Cragside, a leading northern industrialist. Armstrong remodelled much of the castle to his taste, employing the services of Charles Ferguson of Carlisle, work criticised by some architectural historians. Bamburgh Castle is open to the public.

Other points of interest include the memorial to the heroine, Grace Darling (1815-42), who died of consumption and is buried in the local churchyard. Darling, the daughter of a lighthouse keeper on the Farne Islands, had been catapulted to celebrity status as a result of courage displayed in the early hours of 7 September 1838. In bad weather, she valiantly helped her father to row out and rescue members of a ship that had floundered near Longstone Lighthouse. Of her rise to fame, both at home and abroad, Hugh Cunningham comments: 'The speed with which the contemporary media took up her story and the prominence they gave to it is astonishing. Before the 1830s were out, she was the subject of books, plays, panoramas, songs and pottery figurines.'

Bamburgh Parish Church, St Aidan's, lies on the western fringe of the village beside the road leading towards Budle Bay. It is believed to occupy the former site of a wooden chapel where St Aidan died in 651. The church contains some fabric that evidently belonged to a stone predecessor. The present nave, however, either dates from the late 12th or early 13th century

whereas the chancel, the most attractive part of the building, was built in around 1230 and in common with other medieval chancels in the county is long and aisleless.

Opposite: Bamburgh Castle, arguably the most eye-catching building in Northumberland
Top: Bamburgh Parish Church
Above: Memorial to Grace Darling

BERWICK UPON TWEED,
A FASCINATING BORDER TOWN

Berwick, the northernmost town in England, lies at the mouth of the River Tweed near the border with Scotland, and evidently began as a rural settlement. Its name may derive from words that meant 'barley farm.'

In the late 11th century, following the accession of Edgar I of Scotland in 1097, within whose realm Berwick lay, the settlement was referred to as 'the noble village of Berwick.' One of Edgar's successors was his brother David, who ruled Scotland in the years 1124-53, and Berwick prospered during this period. In fact, even before his accession, David (who controlled southern Scotland) had granted Berwick the status of a royal burgh. David is also credited with founding Berwick Castle, a fortress located on a commanding position on the northwest fringe of the town and overlooking the Tweed.

Although Berwick was burnt in early 1216 by John, England's king, during a period of Anglo-Scottish conflict, for most of the 13th century Berwick flourished and was the most prosperous town in Scotland. The borough encompassed about 125 acres (50ha), although about a third of this area was scarcely developed. Wool, grain and salmon were exported from the port and the town's inhabitants included a group of Flemish merchants.

An indication of Berwick's stature is the fact that by the late 13th century 15 religious houses had a presence in the town. For example, the Abbey of Melrose possessed property here. The most significant religious connection was that of the friars, who favoured basing their operations in urban centres. There were five friaries in the thriving borough. These included a Carmelite house founded in 1270 and located at or near the site of today's Governor's House in Palace Street East.

A dramatic phase in Berwick's history subsequently began following the outbreak of war with England. On Friday, 30 March 1296, a powerful army appeared on the scene under the command of England's formidable king, Edward I. Warships, accompanying the army, moved into action by sailing into the harbour. The foremost ran aground and was surrounded and burnt by the Scots. The next two ships also caught fire but their crews escaped in small boats. Demoralised, the rest of the fleet withdrew. Trumpets then sounded the advance for Edward's army and, because Berwick did not possess strong defences, the English were soon in control. According to English sources, the only serious resistance was offered by a body of Flemish merchants. Berwick's women and children were allowed to leave, but the town's menfolk were slaughtered. They 'fell like autumn leaves' and the bodies were thrown down wells or dumped into the sea. The English also gained possession of Berwick Castle, whose commander surrendered.

After sacking Berwick, Edward began to rebuild the town and provide stronger defences. The latter, extending 2½ miles (4km), were completed in the early 14th century following the king's death. Berwick was retaken by the Scots in 1318, and remained under their control until it surrendered to the English following a siege in 1333. Afterwards, control of the strategically important town and castle passed back and forth on several occasions. Finally, in the summer of 1482 Berwick was captured by English troops, led by the future Richard III, and has remained part of England ever since.

The defences were dilapidated when Henry VIII became king in 1509. In later years, his government took measures to strengthen the town by providing artillery strongpoints. But it was Henry's daughter, Queen Elizabeth, who made a much greater impact. In the early years of her reign, Berwick was strengthened by the construction of the best early modern town defences

Berwick Castle

in Great Britain. Work on the fortifications, comprising a wall 20ft (6.1m) high, fronted by a ditch 150ft (46m) wide, and complete with projecting bastions and artillery, began in 1558 when a Scottish invasion was feared. Progress continued until 1570 when work stopped before the scheme had been completed. Consequently, the south and west sides of the town continued to use the medieval town wall. An earth embankment, intended as part of the Elizabethan defences, was finally added behind the Elizabethan wall in the years 1639-53.

The new defences enclosed a smaller acreage than those of the medieval period (one third of the town's former area lay outside the Elizabethan fortifications) for Berwick was a shadow of its 13th century heyday. The shrunken population numbered around 1,500 people, many of whom lived in squalid conditions. Moreover, in the spring of 1603, James VI of Scotland succeeded to the throne of England as James I, and following his accession a large-scale reduction in the military presence ensued.

The imposing Elizabethan defences

James, while en route to London in the year of his accession, briefly visited Berwick. With a degree of trepidation, he then left the town by crossing the Tweed on a wooden bridge that did not inspire confidence. The unsatisfactory structure, which fell down in 1608, was duly replaced in the years 1611-24 by a stone bridge that still stands and is now only crossed by vehicles leaving Berwick.

During the Civil Wars of the 1640s, Berwick was garrisoned by troops opposed to King Charles I. Shortly thereafter, in 1649 a member of the region's gentry, Colonel George Fenwick of Brinkburn was appointed Berwick's governor. He was responsible for erecting one of the town's most notable buildings, Holy Trinity Church. Located in the northernmost part of the town, the place of worship was constructed in the early 1650s.

Fenwick went to his grave in 1657. In the same year, Berwick purchased property directly across the River Tweed, namely the manor of Tweed-mouth and Spittal, bought from the Earl of Suffolk for £570.

In the early 18th century, in the aftermath of the unsuccessful Jacobite rebellion of 1715, Berwick was provided with some of the country's first purpose-built barracks, built near Holy Trinity. The accommodation, designed to house 636 officers and men, comprised two three-storey blocks facing each other across a square. Their construction was ordered in 1717 and building work was completed in 1721. Berwick's townsfolk welcomed the barracks, as troops had previously been billeted in local alehouses. The architect was evidently Nicholas Hawksmoor, a former colleague of Sir John Vanbrugh, and a very capable architect in his own right. An additional block was erected in mid century.

Fishing was still an important part of Berwick's economy and in the mid 1720s Daniel Defoe, whilst travelling through Britain, noted of Berwick that 'the chief trade I found here was in corn and salmon.'

The town's most notable building dating from the 18th century, a new town hall, was erected between 1750 and 1761. It stands in the main thoroughfare, Marygate, and the town gaol was located on the upper floor.

The first recorded shipbuilding yard at Berwick was founded by Arthur Byram in 1751 (a venture that remained in the hands of his family for well over a century) and by the 1790s the yard, then known as 'Gowans', was producing an average of four ships a year. Vessels made on the river included Berwick smacks, fast ships designed to carry salmon to London.

During the second half of the 18th century, considerable development took place at Berwick. Hence, John Fuller described the town as follows: 'The houses, particularly in the High-Street and Hide-Hill, are, for the most part, three stories in height; and many of them are not only highly commodious within, but those of modern erection are handsomely fronted.' He also states that 'A considerable number of the Shops exhibit an appearance of neatness and elegance greatly superior to what they did a few years ago.'

In 1808 a petition to parliament declared that 'the Harbour of Berwick is a place of considerable and increasing resort for Ships and Vessels trading to and from the same.' Agricultural produce was shipped in large quantities. Furthermore, in the first decade of the century approximately 350 tons of salmon were exported annually.

The petition led to an Act of Parliament, granting permission to build a pier (to replace a decaying one built in 1557) and make other harbour improvements. Construction work on the new pier, half a mile (0.8km) long, began in 1810 and concluded in 1826 when a lighthouse was built at the end of the structure.

Ironically, by then Berwick's fortunes had waned. For one thing, the Scottish port of Leith was attracting much of the trade that would have been shipped from the Tweed. Of Berwick's new pier, in 1826 an anonymous commentator observed: 'this pier, which promised so much to improve the harbour, has lessened the trade of the place, by the harbour dues being increased to defray the expense of its erection.' The structure was also blamed for a drop in the number of salmon entering the Tweed.

Shortly thereafter, under the Municipal Corporations Act of 1835, Tweedmouth and Spittal became part of Berwick. Later still, in August 1850, the imposing Royal Border Bridge was opened by Queen Victoria and Prince Albert. Designed by Robert Stephenson, it was built to carry a railway—today's East Coast Main Line—across the Tweed. The bridge replaced a temporary wooden viaduct that had enabled trains to cross the river for a couple of years. Berwick Station was also erected in the 1840s and part of the long-disused castle was destroyed in the process.

In the 1860s, a visitor named John Murray was not impressed with Berwick. He recorded that the town 'of 8613 inhabitants, has a dismal, dreary, dirty appearance. The Salmon Fishery formerly brought some prosperity to the town, but it is no longer very productive…The glory of Berwick has departed.'

A significant development occurred in the following decade, when Berwick's harbour was transformed by the construction of a dock at Tweedmouth. Work began in 1873 and the dock opened in the autumn of 1876. It encompassed 3½ acres (1.4ha) of water and was provided with, among other things, a steam crane and a coal staithe. Stafford Linsley aptly comments that the dock 'was a considerable improvement to the harbour facilities on the Tweed.'

Shortly after this, Berwick's barracks became the depot of the King's Own Scottish Borderers, a role that lasted from 1881 until 1964. The regimental museum is located at the barracks, now in the care of English Heritage.

Robert Stephenson's spectacular Royal Border Bridge

In the 1920s, Berwick's infrastructure was enhanced by the construction of the Royal Tweed Bridge, just upstream from the bridge built in the days of James I. The concrete bridge opened in 1928 and carried the A1 (the coastal road between London and Edinburgh) across the river. However, as a result of a bypass constructed in the 1980s, traffic using that road no longer passes through Berwick.

The town attracted enemy attention in World War Two. Spittal was the most badly affected area. The worst incident occurred in the early hours of 3 June 1941 when 11 people were killed in Sunnyside Crescent, Spittal, and seven others died on the north side of the river. In all, during the war, 21 civilians lost their lives as a result of air raids on the town, whose defences included anti-aircraft guns mounted on the Elizabethan walls.

Turning to sport, Berwick Rangers Football club was founded in the early 1880s. The club has been based at Shielfield Park on the south side of the river since 1954. The following year, Berwick Rangers was admitted to the Scottish Football League—a unique status for an English club. Severe financial difficulties have blighted the club, which almost went bankrupt in 1989. Happier occasions included a thrilling run in the Scottish Cup in 1967 when Rangers reached the fourth round, having clocked up a memo-

Opposite: The 17th century bridge leading to the heart of Berwick.
The spire of the town hall can also be seen

rable victory over Glasgow Rangers at Shielfield in the previous round, a match watched by the club's record attendance figure of 13,365.

In the centre of Berwick lies the Maltings Theatre and Cinema, the largest performing arts venue between Newcastle and Edinburgh: it was officially opened on 4 April 1990 by HRH Princess Margaret and Peter Palumbo, the Chairman of the Arts Council. The heart of the purpose-built complex is the 311-seat main house theatre, which caters for a wide variety of tastes, and in recent years over 50,000 tickets have been sold annually. On the upper floor, lies the Maltings Kitchen, a fully licensed restaurant and café.

In addition to branches of stores such as W.H. Smith and Tesco, the town possesses a number of good independent shops. One such is Geo. C. Grieves Ltd in Church Street (at the bottom of Marygate) a bookseller and stationer that has occupied the premises for over a hundred years.

Berwick's population is approximately 11,500 strong. Although the days of great importance are long over, the town certainly ranks among the finest in Northumberland and is undoubtedly the most picturesque.

CHARLES AVISON,
NEWCASTLE'S FORMER MAESTRO

I n the mid 1730s a talented Geordie named Charles Avison returned to Tyneside after a brief absence in the capital and rapidly enhanced the region's music scene. Among other things, he proceeded to make his name as a composer. Indeed, the *New Grove Dictionary of Music and Musicians* describes him as 'the most important English concerto composer of the 18th century.'

The composer by Charles Lindo, 1761

The son of a local musician, Charles Avison was born at Newcastle on 16 February 1709. As a young man, he travelled to London—he did so in the early 1730s—where he received instruction from a highly admired Italian violinist and composer, Francesco Geminiani.

Avison returned to Newcastle in 1735, where he was appointed organist of St John's Church. Advancement soon followed. In October 1736 he acquired the premier musical post in the town, that of organist of St Nicholas Church. Furthermore, in order to support himself and his family (he had married a local woman fairly soon after returning to Newcastle) he supplemented his income by teaching.

In addition, Avison greatly enlivened music in Newcastle by holding regular subscription concerts. These were performed by an orchestra of professional and amateur musicians, some of whom were gentry. The first series of concerts, held in the Assembly Room on Westgate Road, commenced on Wednesday 1 October 1735 (a day earlier than first advertised) and ran, on a fortnightly basis, into the early months of the following year. Among other things, Avison also held mid-year Race or Assize Week concerts at Newcastle and, in the late 1750s, began to hold a programme of short-lived concerts on the first Thursday of every month from April to August.

Tyneside's music maestro became relatively prosperous. Hence from 1763 he lived at Green Court, a good address near St Andrew's Church in the northwest quarter of Newcastle. He died there seven years later and was laid to rest in the churchyard. Of him, David Hughes has aptly noted: 'Avison, single-handedly, made Newcastle England's greatest provincial music centre of the time.'

Moreover, he wrote a substantial quantity of enjoyable music—his first printed works appeared in 1737—that struck a chord with people throughout the land. Following his death, the music was neglected. Thankfully, however, recent years have witnessed a notable and well-deserved revival. This has been led by the Avison Ensemble, formed in 1984 by a Newcastle-born cellist and musical director, Gordon Dixon. The ensemble has made CD recordings of Avison's music and has held numerous concerts in Newcastle and further afield. For example, it has done so at Alnwick, Berwick upon Tweed, Hexham and Morpeth.

Avison's grave in Newcastle

CRAGSIDE & ITS REMARKABLE CREATOR

C ragside lies in the heart of Northumberland and is one of the county's main tourist attractions. It comprises a remarkable country house and a splendid estate carved out of barren moorland and both owe their existence to a fascinating character, William George Armstrong.

Armstrong was born into a middle-class family at Newcastle in 1810 and was not a robust child. Consequently, for the sake of his health, he sometimes journeyed to the more salubrious location of Rothbury, beside the River Coquet. Indeed, his earliest recollections were of time spent there where he paddled in the river, gathered pebbles and climbed among rocks overlooking the town.

At his father's bidding, William Armstrong proceeded to study law and became a partner in a firm of Newcastle solicitors in 1833. However a lawyer's life had little appeal, for he was far more interested in science and engineering. He was, for example, fascinated by the subject of hydraulics—harnessing water power as effectively as possible.

Therefore, at the beginning of 1847 the reluctant solicitor (who had married in 1835) abandoned his legal career and established W.G. Armstrong & Company, an enterprise founded with several partners. The firm, based at Elswick on the western outskirts of Newcastle, went from strength to strength and manufactured a wide variety of equipment and machinery, including hydraulic cranes that Armstrong had invented. Subsequently, he also designed the world's most up-to-date artillery, which was thus also

A statue of William Armstrong near Haymarket in Newcastle

made at Elswick and by 1863 Armstrong's firm employed more people in engineering than any other in Newcastle.

Late that year, Sir William Armstrong (he had been knighted in 1859) purchased 20 acres (8.1ha) of land in the Debdon Valley near Rothbury, and soon built himself a substantial lodge there, a suitable residence for shooting or fishing parties. It was the start of what would ultimately become an estate covering over 1,700 acres (678ha). The lodge was built on a ledge of rock on a craggy hillside overlooking the Debdon burn, and so Armstrong named the house 'Cragside.'

The main facade of Cragside

Thereafter, he employed the up-and-coming architect, Norman Shaw, to transform the building into a more imposing residence and by the mid 1870s Armstrong—whose industrial interests now included the construction of ships on Tyneside—had made Cragside his main residence. Shaw's last phase of work on the mansion ended in 1884, the year in which the house and estate were visited by the future Edward VII, and his wife Princess Alexandra.

The royal couple spent three nights at Cragside and must have found much to intrigue them. Certainly, it was no ordinary estate. As Andrew Saint comments, at Cragside Sir William had 'created the most extensive and ingenious hydraulic system ever found on a country estate.' Among other things, it powered a sawmill and farm machinery, pumped water and, from 1878, ran a dynamo providing electric light. In fact, Cragside was the first house in the world lit by water-generated electricity!

Sir William was made the first Baron Armstrong of Cragside in 1887. He died at his beloved home on 27 December 1900, shortly after his 90th birthday, and was laid to rest beside his wife, who had died several years earlier, in a corner of the churchyard of Rothbury Parish Church, close to the River Coquet.

Of Lord Armstrong, the *Dictionary of National Biography* aptly noted that his 'name will always stand high among the most illustrious men of the nineteenth century, who have rendered it memorable for the advance in scientific knowledge and in the adaptation of natural forces to the service of mankind.'

Opposite: Hadrian's Wall west of Housesteads Roman Fort

HADRIAN'S WALL & ARBEIA

Hadrian's Wall is by far the most famous and impressive reminder of the days when most of Britain was under Roman rule. Their conquest had commenced in AD 43 when a formidable army landed in Kent, and by around the year 80 the North East had also come under Roman dominance. Indeed, Roman troops advanced deep into what is now Scotland.

By the early years of the 2nd century though, Rome had fallen back to the Tyne-Solway isthmus and it was here that work on building Hadrian's Wall began in the early 120s. This vast task was undertaken at the behest of Hadrian, who had become emperor five years earlier.

The Wall was built to mark the northern frontier of the province, and was 73 miles (117km) long. Some sections were around 7ft (2.13m) thick, whereas others had a width of 10ft (3m). Moreover, the height varied from around 15 to 20ft (4.57 to 6.1m). At regular intervals, the Wall was provided with turrets and small forts. The latter had two gateways, one of which opened through the Wall, and were located every Roman mile, approximately 1,617 yards (1,479m); hence the modern term, 'milecastles'. These fortlets were likely garrisoned by around 25 men. However, several major forts were also part of the defensive scheme, and the consensus of opinion is that they were an afterthought, added when the construction

programme was already underway. Among such forts were Chesters (built to guard a bridge carrying the Wall across the North Tyne), Carrawburgh, Housesteads and Carvoran.

In addition, the frontier was strengthened by digging a ditch along the northern side of the Wall, except where the steep nature of the terrain made this impossible or unnecessary, as was the case for example at Housesteads. Furthermore the *Vallum*, a large ditch, flanked by banks, was dug behind the line of the Wall in a strip of cleared ground. However, no trace of this feature has been found between Newcastle and Wallsend, presumably because the River Tyne served as an effective barrier. Causeways at forts enabled the *Vallum* to be crossed. Traffic through the Wall was also allowed, under the supervision of members of the garrison.

Roman forts were usually built to a standard plan. Enclosed by one or more external defensive ditches, they were shaped like a playing card, and had a gate in each of the four straight sides, angle towers in the rounded corners, and other internal towers at intervals between. The largest buildings were the *principia*—the headquarters—and the *prætoria*, the commanding officer's well-appointed residence. Some of the forts partly projected from the line of the Wall—Chesters is a case in point—and had gates that enabled soldiers to have ready access to the land beyond the frontier where garrisons were stationed in outpost forts such as High Rochester and Risingham.

On the other hand, some of the region's forts—the most well known is Vindolanda—lay a few miles to the south of Hadrian's Wall and were located along a Roman road that predated the Wall and likewise crossed the Tyne-Solway isthmus. From the 160s, this road was supplemented by the Military Way. Constructed between the *Vallum* and the Wall, the new road linked the forts etc along the frontier and provided speedier communication than had been possible hitherto. Provision of the Military Way also entailed replacing the bridge at Chesters with a much more imposing structure to carry the road over the North Tyne.

The bulk of the manpower involved in constructing Hadrian's Wall had come from three Roman legions, prestigious units recruited from Roman citizens. The troops who actually garrisoned the Wall were auxiliaries, soldiers drawn from subject peoples of the empire who could look forward to being granted Roman citizenship following 25 years of service. One such unit, of Germanic origin, was *cohors I Tungrorum milliaria* (the 'first cohort of Tungrians a thousand strong'), present at Housesteads by at least AD 200. Germanic names found at the fort indicate that the unit may well have continued to recruit, into the late 3rd century, some of its members from the Tungrians' homeland in present day southern Belgium and Holland.

In common with the other Roman forts, Housesteads was associated with a civil settlement (*vicus*) that developed outside its walls. Here members of the garrison relaxed and spent part of their wages at taverns, shops and brothels.

Opposite: A milecastle on Hadrian's Wall

Worship featured prominently in the lives of the soldiers garrisoning the Wall and one of the numerous deities that had devotees was Mithras, a Persian god whose cult had reached Rome in the 1st century BC. The cult of Mithras was reserved for men and insisted on strict adherence to discipline and integrity. Secrecy was a keynote of the cult, which was popular among army officers. The remains of a Mithraic temple lie just outside the fort at Carrawburgh and Mithraism evidently also was practised elsewhere along the frontier at Newcastle and Wallsend.

The Emperor Hadrian died in 138 and his successor, Antoninus Pius, ordered troops to reoccupy southern Scotland. Consequently, the Antonine Wall was erected between the Firth of Forth and the Clyde. But its existence proved short-lived, for in around 163 Hadrian's Wall resumed its role as the northern frontier and was subjected to serious attacks as the 2nd century drew to a close.

Moreover, in about 163 a fort was built at South Shields where much of the food and other items, such as pottery, used by troops garrisoning the Wall, were landed after being transported by sea. The Romans' connection with the locality was well established and there is reason to believe that a fort had first been erected at South Shields in the late 1st century. The fort built in around 163, covered just over 4 acres (1.6ha) and apparently initially accommodated approximately 480 infantry and 120 cavalry.

Arbeia, looking across the headquarters building towards a reconstructed gateway

Subsequently, in the early 3rd century, Emperor Septimius Severus decided to reoccupy southern Scotland. Important changes thus occurred at Arbeia—the Roman fort at South Shields. Evidently, as part of the preparations made for the emperor's northern campaigns of 208-10, the fort was enlarged to over five acres (5.2ha) and most of the buildings were demolished and replaced by granaries. The fort therefore became a supply base and storage capacity was soon increased by the construction of additional granaries. Owing to the extra storage capacity, the fort could hold approximately six months' supply of grain.

Severus died at York in 211, whereupon the Romans abandoned Scotland. Thereafter, Arbeia served as a supply base for Hadrian's Wall and garrisons manning outpost forts to the north. In around 300, the fort was attacked and seriously damaged by fire and large-scale demolition and reconstruction thus took place; work that included converting eight of the granaries into barracks.

Hadrian's Wall and Arbeia evidently continued to be held by the Romans until the early 5th century—Roman rule in Britain ceased in around 409—when the native population was left to its own devices. Hence, Roman forts and other installations were either abandoned or put to other use as warlords established local spheres of power.

Over the centuries the Roman legacy in the region has been a source of fascination to many. In the 18th century, for example, Hadrian's Wall attracted the keen interest of a number of visitors and antiquaries, including the Scot, Sir John Clerk of Penicuik who visited the Wall in the spring of 1724. Among other things, he noted that 'Between Harley Hill and Halton Shields all the works are very conspicuous and in a plain for near a mile they make … a magnificent appearance.' Continuing westward, Clerk reached Housesteads, which was occupied by a poor farming family. Of the place, he wrote: 'In viewing it I thought I was come amongst the ruins of an old Grecian or Asiatic city…. The length of this city is about 800 yards and the breadth about 400 … though it is probable by other ruins near to it that it has been much larger.' Since Clerk's visit, archaeological excavations at Housesteads have uncovered the most complete example of a Roman fort visible in Britain and the adjoining civil settlement.

Hadrian's Wall is a World Heritage Site.

HEXHAM,
AN HISTORIC MARKET TOWN

Hexham lies in Tynedale and is located on elevated ground a short distance from the south bank of the Tyne. It is a fascinating and attractive place that has much to interest visitors, with a vibrant heritage that dates back to the late 7th century when a colourful figure named Wilfrid founded a monastery here in the early 670s. Wilfrid brought masons and other craftsmen from abroad to construct the monastic church and buildings. Stones from the Roman site at Corbridge (a few miles downstream) were used in the construction programme, and a fascinating fragment of Wilfrid's church still survives, namely an underground crypt that contained prized relics and lay beneath the high altar.

The crypt now lies below the nave of Hexham Abbey, an imposing church that dominates the town. The church was built to serve a community of Augustinian canons that was founded at Hexham in around 1113 and lasted until 1537 when the monastery was closed by officers of Henry VIII. Most of the fabric of the church dates from 1180 or later. Indeed, the nave, the westernmost part of the building, was erected in the early 20th century but incorporates medieval fabric.

Hexham Abbey lies on the west side of a marketplace (which now largely serves as a car park) and faces another old structure, the Moothall. This robust building, erected in around 1400, stands on the east side of the marketplace and was partly used as a courtroom. The Moothall is pierced by a vaulted passageway. This gave access from the marketplace to the 'Archbishop's enclosure', an administrative complex that included Hexham Gaol. The order to build the gaol was given in the summer of 1330 and it was erected to incarcerate prisoners seized in Hexhamshire—a substantial swathe of country mostly located south of the River Tyne. By the 16th century, though, the gaol also held captives from further afield, as was true of Border Reivers from wayward North Tynedale and Redesdale, Northumberland's most troublesome valleys. However, the gaol's level of security was not always high and breakouts sometimes occurred, in some cases with the connivance of guards. The gaol served as a prison until the 1820s. It now houses a museum (there is an entrance fee) dedicated to local history.

When the gaol was built, Hexham and its shire were governed by the Archbishop of York and his officials, a state of affairs that had existed since the late 11th century. The archbishop's control of secular matters lasted until 1545 when it passed into the hands of the Crown and before long, in the early 1570s, the shire became part of Northumberland. Ecclesiastically, though, Hexham and its shire (now part of the diocese of Newcastle) remained part of the archdiocese of York until 1837.

A stone's throw from the gaol, stands an eye-catching building that was erected in 1684. It was built to house Hexham Grammar School, an institution founded almost a century earlier, in 1599, under a charter from Elizabeth I. The school's governing body comprised local gentry and merchants. In addition to religious instruction, emphasis was placed on learning Latin and Greek—in the early 20th century, a replacement grammar school opened elsewhere in the town.

Hexham's economy included tanning, an unsavoury business, and from the 14th century, in order to safeguard the town's drinking water, it was decreed that tanneries should be located beyond the limits of the urban area. Consequently, tanning was practised beside the Cockshaw Burn on the northwestern fringe of Hexham. In time, though, as the industry expanded, it was also undertaken closer to the town centre. Hence in 1661 it was ordered that no inhabitants were to wash animal intestines 'in the west burn called the Abbey Garth Burn or the Cockshaw Burn [located even further west], or shall wash any filthy things in either of the same burns until they come to George Leadbitter's house being the nethermost house in the town upon pain of 6s. 8d.'

A century later, in 1761, Hexham was the location of a riot that occurred when tensions were running high over compulsory service in the militia. A large number of people from the town and surrounding area flocked to a protest meeting at the marketplace and bloodshed ensued when a clash

Hexham Abbey from the south

occurred with troops who had been deployed in the town. In all, 52 civilians lost their lives.

Hexham was well known as a centre of glovemaking, which occurred from at least the Tudor period. In 1823, there were 11 glove manufacturers in the town and, according to the local historian, Andrew White, some 23,500 dozen pairs of gloves were made annually by a workforce that comprised 110 men and boys as leather dressers and cutters, whereas 1,000 women sewed material at home. Sadly, though, by this date foreign competition was soon to almost wipe out Hexham's glovemaking industry.

Turning to other matters, in the mid 1830s traffic by rail commenced when the Blaydon-Hexham section of the developing Newcastle and Carlisle Railway (completed in 1838) began to operate. Consequently, in 1834 lead started to be carried along the line from Hexham to refineries at Blaydon. Passenger traffic commenced the following year.

Of Hexham, in 1853 an official report by Robert Rawlinson noted: 'in no town of a parallel population have I found more filth, overcrowding and general neglect.' One of the streets, Gilesgate (located northwest of the marketplace) was 'even more noxious than all the other parts, with its thickly-populated houses, no privies, no drainage, and stagnant pools. In one case the drainage was so bad that all the filth oozed through the house walls and wet the beds.'

The following year, a Board of Health was formed and various measures ensued. These included providing every house with piped water in the 1860s, and installing a system of sewerage drains in the following decade. Nevertheless, mortality rates did not witness a significant improvement. Indeed, infant mortality generally rose. In 1851 the figure for children under one year of age was 119 per thousand live births but by the turn of the century it peaked at 141.

On a happier note, in the first decade of the 20th century the Gem Cinema, which overlooked the marketplace, was founded. Moreover, in 1911 the Abbey Grounds—located immediately south and west of the historic church—were opened as a public park. Furthermore, in 1920 the Hexham Entertainment Company converted part of a building on Beaumont Street, which faces westward towards the park, into what became known as the Queen's Hall Cinema.

Beaumont Street, named after the lords of the manor of Hexham, was laid out in the mid 1860s and here one finds, among other things, Hexham Library and the offices of the *Hexham Courant*, a newspaper founded in 1864.

On the other hand, several other streets date from medieval times. This is true of St Mary's Chare and Fore Street, located in the heart of the town centre, south of the marketplace. The former, which has access to the marketplace via an archway, is the location of Cogito Bookshop, one of Hexham's most appealing shops, an award-winning family business founded in 2001 by Alan Grint and his wife, Julia. Fore Street also contains a bookshop,

The Moothall   The former grammar school

The abbey viewed from the northwest

St Mary's Chare, one of Hexham's oldest streets

Waterstones, and branches of other national chains such as Holland & Barrett. The street is also adjoined by Beales, Hexham's department store. Previously known as Robbs, the store developed from a shop founded in 1819 by William Robb and was saved from closure when it was purchased by Beales in the summer of 2010.

All in all, Hexham is an attractive place in which to live. It certainly appealed to the Cambridge-educated historian, Tom Corfe (1928-2006) who settled in the town in 1986, where he breathed new life into the local history society, served as a guide at the abbey, and penned a fine concise history entitled *Hexham Heritage*.

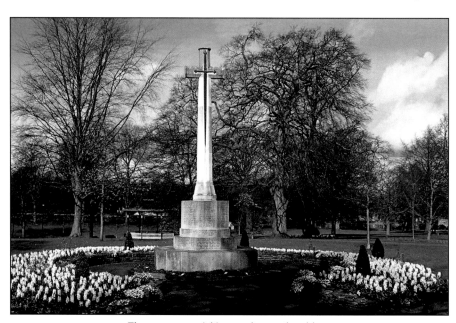

The war memorial in a park near the abbey

HOLY ISLAND

Holy Island lies a mile or so off the coast of Northumberland and at low tide is connected to the mainland by a causeway.

Upon reaching the island, which is also known as Lindisfarne, the road curves around the western shoreline en route to the only village, and for part of the route the road skirts past extensive sand dunes that have developed in the last few hundred years.

Just to the south of the village, lies the parish church, St Mary's. This mostly dates from the early 13th century and was erected to serve a parish that included townships on the mainland, a state of affairs that lasted into the 19th century.

The church likely contains fabric dating from Anglo-Saxon times when a famous monastery was located on the island. In AD 635 a Christian missionary named Aidan was permitted to found a monastery on Lindisfarne by King Oswald of Northumbria. Initially, the monastery was a humble affair, with a roughly thatched timber church that was only replaced by a more imposing structure following Aidan's death in 651. The monastery is famous for its links with St Cuthbert (d. 687) who was a member of the monastic community and also briefly served as the Bishop of Lindisfarne; and for the magnificent *Lindisfarne Gospels*, a masterpiece that dates from the early 8th century.

St Mary's, the parish church

The monastery is also famous because it was bloodily sacked by the Vikings in 793—an event that heralded the onset of the Viking era—and almost a century later the monks abandoned the vulnerable site after another Viking assault and never returned.

Subsequently, in the early 12th century, Benedictine monks from Durham Cathedral Priory established a monastery on the abandoned site. Lindisfarne Priory was a daughter house of Durham and was manned by monks from there. The cell was small and double figures were seldom reached.

The ruined church of the medieval priory

During the 14th century, Holy Island served as a harbour for royal purveyors of goods in transit to English armies campaigning north of the border. Fear that this might lead to Scottish retaliation was perhaps a factor that contributed to the monks' decision to fortify their monastery. Among other things, the church was thus provided with low-pitched roofs and battlemented parapets.

Lindisfarne Priory was dissolved in 1537 during the Dissolution of the Monasteries, but much of the church survives, as do substantial traces of the monastic quarters that lay around a cloister to the south.

The most eye-catching feature of the island is, however, Lindisfarne Castle, a fortress erected on an outcrop of the Great Whin Sill in the mid 16th century and from where artillery could be used to defend the harbour. The last garrison left in 1819 and the castle fell into a sorry state thereafter. It was brought back to life in the early 20th century by Edward Hudson, the founder of *Country Life* magazine. He bought the derelict stronghold in 1902 and employed the architect, Edwin Lutyens, to restore and remodel the castle so that it could be a country retreat, work that continued until 1912. One of Hudson's later guests was the acerbic Lytton Strachey, who observed that the building was 'all timid Lutyens…not a comfortable

Opposite: Lindisfarne Castle

place, by any means.' Strachey did, nevertheless, appreciate the magnificent location. By 1944 the castle was owned by a banker named Sir Edward de Stein who gave it to the National Trust.

A short distance beyond the castle, lie disused limekilns that were built in the 1860s by a Scottish firm. Limestone quarried on the island was drawn along a waggonway by horses to the kilns, and burnt lime was then conveyed along another waggonway to jetties located west of the castle. Production ceased before 1896.

Visitors can also enjoy the island's natural attractions. These include sandy beaches and an abundance of birdlife, for in the autumn wildfowl and waders arrive in large numbers to winter here.

The village also has places of interest. These include the *Ship Inn*, which is located on the main street and dates from the 18th century. Formerly known as the *Northumberland Arms*, it was thoroughly renovated and refurbished in 1995 and given its present name. The village is also the location of the Lindisfarne Centre, whose exhibits include electronic 'Turning the Page' copies of the famous *Lindisfarne Gospels* provided by the British Library. Another attraction is St Aidan's Winery, whose shop opened in 1968 and attracts over 200,000 visitors annually. The winery produces Lindisfarne Mead, a unique alcoholic fortified wine whose ingredients include honey acquired from various sources worldwide.

Holy Island is steeped in history and a delightful place.

'LET THERE BE LIGHT!',
THE STORY OF SOUTER LIGHTHOUSE

'After leaving the Tyne at night we stood off from Souter Point to observe the light from the sea, and it certainly surpassed in brilliancy any I have ever seen, being so bright that at a distance of several miles well-defined shadows were cast upon…deck.'

So wrote an American expert on lighthouses, Major George Elliot, of Souter Lighthouse shortly after it came into operation in 1871. Elliot had good reason to feel impressed for the lighthouse, on the coast between Sunderland and South Shields, produced a beam of 700,000 candlepower.

Souter Lighthouse (pronounced 'Sooter') was built to protect shipping plying the sea between Sunderland and the Tyne. Despite the advent of the railway, in the middle decades of the 19th century the number of ships sailing along the coast was increasing. For one thing, transporting bulk cargoes by sea was more profitable than alternative forms of doing so. One such cargo was coal. It was shipped in considerable quantities and much of the coal was loaded onto vessels at Tyne Dock, a complex that opened on the south bank of the Tyne between South Shields and Jarrow in 1859. Seafaring thus provided many of the region's menfolk with employment.

The occupation was inevitably dangerous. The stretch of water between the Rivers Tyne and Wear had an unenviable reputation. For one thing, submerged rocks—such as Whitburn Steel located off Whitburn and Marsden—added to the hazards sailors faced and numerous vessels foundered between Sunderland and South Shields, inevitably entailing loss of life.

In view of these fatalities, Trinity House, the national lighthouse authority, came under pressure to erect an installation that would improve the woeful state of affairs. In response, it called upon the services of its Chief Engineer, James Douglass, who is best remembered for subsequently designing Eddystone Lighthouse off Plymouth Harbour. Douglass was given the task of designing the required station, one that would supplement lighthouses located at the mouths of the Wear and the Tyne—the oldest of the lighthouses in question dated from 1664, was located on the headland at Tynemouth and lit by a coal fire.

Although born in London in 1826, James Douglass' family ties were with the North East. For instance, his mother was the daughter of a gentleman resident at Winlaton in County Durham. Moreover, Douglass had received part of his education in the county for he attended a school at Blaydon.

In comparison with some of his previous undertakings, working on a land-based lighthouse such as Souter was a straightforward task—some years earlier, when building a lighthouse on a submerged reef between Land's End and the Isles of Scilly, iron stakes, with ropes fastened to them, had had to be driven into the rock so that Douglass and his men would not be swept to their deaths by Atlantic rollers!

The location chosen for Douglass' new venture was Souter Point, midway between the Tyne and the Wear. In the event, another site was decided upon, namely Lizard Point, closer to South Shields. For one thing, the alternative had higher cliffs that would provide the lighthouse with a more prominent setting. A Lizard Point lighthouse already existed in Cornwall. Hence the name 'Souter' was retained for the new lighthouse and the station came into operation at the beginning of 1871.

The lighthouse viewed from the east

The first keeper was Henry Millet, a 39-year-old who was born in Wilt-shire. He was subsequently joined by his wife, Louisa and their children. Millet was still at the lighthouse in 1881, along with his wife and 11 children, most of whom had been born in the preceding decade. Ten years later, however, Henry Millet was resident at a lighthouse on the Isle of Wight.

One of the members of staff in the closing decades of the 19th century was a nephew of the heroine Grace Darling, a young woman who had shot to fame by helping to rescue shipwrecked sailors off the coast of Northum-berland in 1838.

Souter, as Major Elliot noted, was no ordinary lighthouse. The latest technology had been employed to make it as efficient as possible. It was one of the first lighthouses in the world where electricity was used to power the light, and the first lighthouse anywhere lit by an alternating current magneto-electric generator designed by Professor Holmes.

Within the lantern, the room enclosing the light at the top of the tower of the lighthouse, a large rotating octagonal drum with seven vertical lenses on each side, focused the light and greatly increased its strength, thereby producing the extremely powerful beam referred to above that so impressed Major Elliot.

At other lighthouses, half the light cast by the revolving beam was projected inland. Douglass ensured that this did not happen at Souter. He

Souter Lighthouse bathed in evening sunlight against a stormy sky

installed a series of prisms that prevented the light being wasted in such a way. Instead, via the prisms, the light was reflected part of the way down the tower, which is over 75ft (22.8m) high, and through a window in the lower lantern room so that it formed an arc, visible for 6 miles (9.6km), over Sunderland Bay thereby aiding vessels approaching the Wear.

In view of this and its other novel features, one can well understand why Sir Frederick Arrow, the Deputy-Master of Trinity House, declared when Souter opened that 'no lighthouse in any part of the world would bear comparison with it.'

Initially, there was a single foghorn, facing directly out to sea and located on a freestanding building closer to the cliff edge. By the early years of the 20th century, it had been replaced by two foghorns arranged in such a way that they faced up and down the coast. The present trumpet-like horns, angled in the same manner, are of more recent date. When required the foghorns provided a four-second blast every 45 seconds and the sound was audible for miles.

Like other land-based lighthouses, Souter is painted white, with green doors and window sills, and has a black roof. Apart from the foghorn house, the buildings are located on the landward side of the tower and are ranged around a courtyard. In addition to the engine room, boiler house and fuel store etc., the ranges contained six cottages for staff and their families and each cottage was provided with a front garden and a backyard, complete with a wash-house, fuel store and lavatory.

The lighthouse was powered by electricity until 1914, when the machinery was past its best and a major overhaul thus occurred. Among other things, this included switching from electricity to oil, a state of affairs that continued until 1952 when electricity (now supplied by the National Grid) was used once again. It powered 4,500 watt bulbs that produced a beam equivalent to 1.5 million candles!

By the 1980s the number of ships plying the coast had fallen significantly. Hence in 1988 Trinity House decided to close the lighthouse and two years later it was bought by the National Trust. The lighthouse, which still provides aid to seamen via an automatic radio beacon, is open to the public and contains much of interest. Visitors unafraid of heights or enclosed spaces are able to ascend to the lantern where they can examine apparatus and, on clear days, enjoy panoramic views of the coast.

Houses overlooking the North Tyne at Wark

The remote Hartside Farm in the Breamish Valley beneath the Cheviot hills

Dunstanburgh Castle, a stronghold built in the 14th century. It was once owned by John of Gaunt

South Shields town hall, a notable example of Edwardian architecture

Beadnell harbour. The limekilns date from about 1800

MORPETH,
Northumberland's County Town

Located in the valley of the River Wansbeck, Morpeth lies approximately 15 miles (24km) north of Newcastle. The town, which mostly occupies ground north and east of a loop of the river, has existed since the Middle Ages and in 1199 or the following year, its lord, Roger de Merlay was granted a charter by King John. This decreed that the baron and his heirs could have an annual fair at the borough on the feast of St Magdalene (22 July) and a weekly market on Wednesdays.

Nowadays, Morpeth is bypassed by the county's main north-south road, the A1, but for centuries the town lay on the Great North Road, and for most of this period traffic crossed the Wansbeck via a humped-back bridge erected in the 13th century. The central pillar of the bridge still exists and supports a Victorian footbridge.

Other reminders of Morpeth's medieval past also survive. For example, on elevated ground south of the river stands Morpeth Castle, the former stronghold of the de Merlays, for whom the barony of Morpeth was created in the 1090s. Their first castle, a motte and bailey, was probably located on Ha' Hill (closer to the Wansbeck) and was destroyed by King John in early 1216 during a civil war in which the Merlays, like the majority of Northumberland's baronage, opposed the king. John died later that year and likely shortly afterwards the Merlays built a replacement castle. Although the keep no longer exists, sections of the curtain wall survive, as does the mid 14th century gatehouse built at a time when the castle had passed into the hands of the Greystoke family.

Other reminders of medieval Morpeth are the parish church of St Mary the Virgin, and All Saints' chantry. The former, which mostly dates from the 14th century, lies a short distance southwest of the castle and is one of the few churches in the county to still have some medieval glass. Indeed, the east window contains the most important 14th-century stained glass in the county. The chantry, on the other hand, is located on the north side of the Wansbeck beside the town's main thoroughfare, Bridge Street, and was reportedly built in 1296 but some architectural historians think it looks older.

Among other things, the chantry operated a school and it is reasonable to conclude that one of the boys who received instruction there was William Turner, a tanner's son born in Morpeth in around 1508. Turner studied at Cambridge University and on the continent. He was a staunch Protestant and became the Dean of Wells in Somerset. He was also keenly interested in nature and wrote a highly influential three-volume work on plants entitled *A New Herbal* that has justly earned him an honoured place in the history of botany.

William Turner died in London in 1568, by which time John Leland had visited Morpeth (he did so in 1540) and had observed that: 'The town is long and metely well builded with low houses, the streets paved. It is far fairer town than Alnwick.'

Morpeth's chantry closed during this period. As was true of chantries nationwide, it was shut by the government as a result of legislation passed in 1548. Four years later, the premises became the Edward VI Grammar School—an institution partly endowed with the former chantry's property—that moved to other premises in the Victorian era.

The gatehouse of Morpeth Castle

Early in 1644, during the Civil War, Morpeth Castle was captured and garrisoned by Scottish troops allied to parliament. In response, on 10 May, Royalists under the Marquis of Montrose tried and failed to storm the stronghold. Montrose thus began a siege, and cannon proceeded to batter the castle for several days. Hence Montrose 'not only drove the soldiers of the garrison from their defences…but also in many places opened the walls.' The garrison duly capitulated on 29 May and was allowed to leave for Berwick.

In the early 18th century, Morpeth received a new town hall. The building, which faces northward towards the marketplace, was designed by Sir John Vanbrugh. It was paid for by Morpeth's landlord, the Earl of Carlisle (the head of a junior branch of the Howard family) one of whose forebears had acquired Morpeth by marriage into the Dacre family in the mid 16th century.

Although resident elsewhere, the Earls of Carlisle dominated local affairs and usually, at any given time, at least one of the town's MPs (Morpeth had returned two members to parliament since 1553) was a Howard or one of their relations. As a result of the Reform Act of 1832, Morpeth was reduced to a one-seater constituency, albeit covering a much larger area that now included the parish of Bedlington.

Other developments in the 19th century included the founding of a dispensary in Oldgate in 1817 (a street where Admiral Collingwood, Nelson's second-in-command at Trafalgar, had owned a house); and the construction of the county gaol, a building fronted by an imposing 'medieval' courthouse erected in 1822-8 and designed by the celebrated architect John Dobson. In 1881, the gaol was relocated to Newcastle. On the other hand, the courthouse retained that role until 1980.

In 1829-31, moreover, the medieval bridge, which had become unsatisfactory, was replaced by a crossing designed by no less a figure than Thomas Telford. Of the old bridge, the historian John Hodgson had recently observed: 'For the present rapid mode of travelling it is inconvenient and dangerous— the Mail and Wonder coaches having each, within the last 3 years, once carried away the south end of its west battlements, and been thrown with their passengers and horses into the river—fortunately, without loss of life.'

Morpeth's transport network was further enhanced by the arrival of the Newcastle to Berwick Railway in 1847, and the borough thus gained a station, designed by Benjamin Green, located on its southern periphery. The advent of travel by rail was, however, a mixed blessing. For one thing, it added to the problems of the town's long-established cattle market—a central facet of the local economy held in the marketplace and Bridge Street—that had already suffered from increasing competition from a rival market at Newcastle. Although cattle continued to be sold in Morpeth, the heyday was certainly over.

Furthermore, in the mid 19th century Morpeth's chief industries, such as tanning, which Hodgson had described as 'the most staple and important trade of this town', were also in trouble. Indeed, by the 1870s the industry was no longer practised in Morpeth.

The mid century economic woes led to a significant decline in population. Despite the arrival of Irish immigrants, the number of residents in

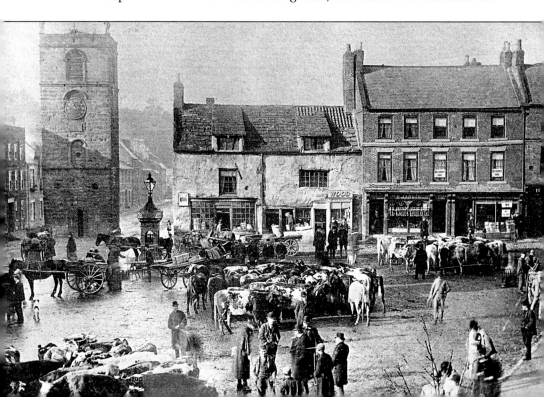

Looking upstream towards Telford's bridge

the period 1841-51 fell by 18 per cent to over 4,300 people, a population that nevertheless included a proportionately larger middle class than was true of some other urban centres.

A positive development occurred in 1866, namely the founding of Swinney Brothers, the town's first engineering works. The factory's first major project involved the construction, in 1869, of the footbridge mentioned above. Swinney's prospered and by 1890 had 130 employees, a dramatic rise from the initial workforce of only eight staff, and numbers subsequently increased. Of the business, which operated in Morpeth until 1985, Phil Huntley comments in issue 89 of *The Northumbrian*: 'Products included lamp-posts, galley stoves and flood gullies.... The start of the firm's innovations came with patents for brick-making machinery in 1876, which was used by brickworks both locally and as far afield as Australia and South Africa.'

By 1891, Morpeth's population was over 5,200 strong. A number of the residents had been attracted to the borough to work in collieries that had opened in the neighbourhood. Ian Willis states in *Northumbrian Panorama* that 'by 1891 miners had become the largest male occupational group' in the town. Nevertheless, the same author comments that 'Morpeth's prosperity primarily depended upon its role as a retail and service centre for its agricultural hinterland.'

In June 1913, Emily Davison, a militant suffragette killed by a horse whilst protesting at that year's Derby, was laid to rest at Morpeth. Her body

Opposite: Selling cattle in the heart of Morpeth, a practice that ceased in 1903

arrived by train and large crowds watched as the cortege travelled from the station to nearby St Mary's Church, where she was interred beside her father.

On a happier note, in 1916 the Countess of Carlisle granted land on the south side of the Wansbeck to the people of Morpeth. Over a decade later, in 1929, this property was opened to the public. Aptly named Carlisle Park, it covers 33 acres (13.35ha) and Morpeth Castle lies within its attractive grounds. A recent feature in the park is the Turner Garden, which bears the name of Morpeth's most famous son and opened at the turn of the millennium.

In 2008, Morpeth was the most badly affected place in Northumberland hit by flooding caused by prolonged heavy rainfall. On Saturday, 6 September, the Wansbeck burst its banks and around 900 homes were flooded. Other property affected included Morpeth Library, which sustained damage to the premises and stock. At the peak of the flood, the volume of water that swept eastward towards the library down Bridge Street (Morpeth's high street) reached a depth of 2ft (0.6m).

Just over a year later, on 12 November 2009, a shopping centre known as the Sanderson Arcade was opened by the actress and TV presenter, Joanna Lumley. The centre, which stands on the site of a rundown predecessor established in the 1950s, contains 27 stores, including a number belonging to national chains. On the other hand, Appleby's Bookshop in Newgate Street is a much-loved independent business that has been based in the same premises since 1884. The shop almost closed in early 2012 as a result of a steep drop in sales caused by lengthy roadworks.

Morpeth has a population of approximately 14,000. It became Northumberland's county town in 1981 when Northumberland County Council, hitherto based in Newcastle, moved to purpose-built premises on the southern outskirts of the town.

Carlisle Park – an attractive feature of the town

MORPETH MUSIC SOCIETY

Morpeth Music Society was formed in 1944 during the dark days of World War Two and was founded in affiliation with the forerunner of the Arts Council. A number of concerts had already been held in the town since 1941 (Kathleen Ferrier was one of the singers involved) and their success had shown that strong support existed in Morpeth and its environs for such music.

Records from 1949 show that the society's membership was over 100 strong, and performers included the acclaimed violinist Ralph Holmes and the bass baritone Owen Brannigan who was born at Annitsford in Northumberland in 1908. Brannigan enjoyed an international career as an opera singer (he was for instance with Sadler's Wells in the years 1944-9) but also performed Northumbrian folk music.

More recent performers have included the pianist Sarah Beth Briggs, who was born in Newcastle upon Tyne in 1972. A prodigious talent, she made her debut when she performed Brahms' *Handel Variations* for the society when only ten years old. She has since enjoyed an international solo career. Moreover, on occasion she performs as a member of the Clarion

The society's commitee and members of the London Concertante in 2009

The society's president Ian Armstrong presenting David Forbes with a certificate

Trio, and did so for the society at a concert held at Morpeth Town Hall on Thursday, 14 December 2006.

The society holds six concerts from October to April, and the usual venue is Morpeth's Methodist Church. The former chairman, Kathy Smith commented: 'We are keen to attract young people to our concerts and to this end we have links with local schools, providing them with complimentary tickets and recently we introduced a scholarship to be awarded each year to a promising music student from one of the local schools.' In 2010, for example, the winner was David Forbes, and the scholarship is provided courtesy of the estate of Dr Eileen Bowler, who taught music at King Edward VI School. Kathy also noted that the 'people of Morpeth and the surrounding areas support us well and we are fortunate to have some very generous sponsors.'

The society continues to flourish and attract outstanding artists. On 2 February, 2012, for instance, the London Haydn Quartet gave an excellent performance of music by Beethoven and Haydn and was joined by Eric Hoeprich to perform Mozart's Clarinet Quintet.

NEWCASTLE UPON TYNE,
A Brief History of the North East's Capital

'I ts identity is singular. A broad and rapid river...over which a strong stone bridge connects it with Gateshead...[is] constantly covered, to the east of the bridge, with shipping of almost every description, and from almost every quarter of the globe....Here is a basis upon which to build piles of golden treasures. Hence may be anticipated the dense population, the bustling mart, the very soul of a commercial spirit, in all its enterprising varieties.'

So wrote the Reverend Thomas Dibdin upon visiting Newcastle in the late 1830s. It was indeed a thriving centre, the most populous town in the region and a place with a long and fascinating history.

Evidently, the site now occupied by Newcastle was not a major focus of human settlement in prehistoric times. On the other hand, in view of the significant number of bronze swords recovered from the river, it did serve as an important religious centre in the period c.1100-700 BC—the late Bronze Age—and perhaps remained the location of ritualistic activity for some time thereafter.

Dramatic changes ensued in the Roman era. During the reign of Emperor Hadrian (AD 117-38) a bridge, the *Pons Aelius*, was built to span the Tyne at Newcastle (it perhaps did so at the site of today's Victorian Swing Bridge) and carried a major road across the river. Hadrian's Wall, which runs across the Tyne-Solway isthmus, was also built. Initially, it ran westward from the vicinity of the *Pons Aelius*, and probably started at a point just downstream. But an eastward extension was soon erected and terminated at Wallsend.

The Roman presence was further strengthened when a fort was constructed on elevated ground overlooking the *Pons Aelius*. The fort is often said to have dated from the Hadrianic period but evidence from archaeological excavations at the site, now occupied by Newcastle's medieval castle, indicate that it was built in the late 2nd or early 3rd century and was certainly in existence by 213. A civil settlement developed outside the fort and lay on ground to the west.

Several generations after Rome abandoned Britain in the early 5th century, the Newcastle area passed under the control of Germanic rulers, the Anglo-Saxons. Moreover, in the 7th century, during the days of the kingdom of Northumbria, missionaries converted the people to Christianity. Later still, in the 8th century, at Newcastle a substantial cemetery was located on the site of the ruined Roman fort to serve as a burial ground for the locality's population, which was evidently rural rather than urban in nature. Evidence also suggests that a church existed on the historic site.

A significant new phase commenced in 1080. Robert Curthose, the eldest son of William the Conqueror, built an earth and timber castle, partly enclosed by a deep ditch, on the same commanding position as the one chosen centuries earlier by the Romans for their fort. A town soon began to develop in the shadow of the royal castle and the settlement was granted borough status at some point during the reign of Henry I (1100-35). From the mid 1090s, at the latest, the community worshipped in a wooden parish church dedicated to St Nicholas. During the 12th century, this was rebuilt in stone. Three subordinate churches, St Andrew's, St John's and All Hallow's (subsequently known as All Saints) were also in existence by the end of that century.

The formidable keep built by Henry II

Likely, shortly after the town of Newcastle began to emerge, a bridge was built to link up with Gateshead on the south side of the river. What is certain is that by 1160 the Tyne was spanned by a stone bridge. Furthermore, within the next decade or so the castle was rebuilt in stone by King Henry II and provided with an imposing and sophisticated keep. Further changes to the fortress, including the construction of a formidable new entrance, the Black Gate, were made in the mid 13th century by Henry III.

Newcastle, by 1300, was emphatically the leading borough in the North East and was home to around 7,500 people. The town's prosperity was mostly derived from seaborne trade, especially the shipment of wool. Coal, too, was shipped from the borough but was of little importance to the local economy until the mid 14th century.

As the town expanded, major reclamation took place along the riverside. This process had begun as early as the late 12th century, and would continue into the Tudor period. As a result, the width of the Tyne was reduced by almost 40 feet (12.1m) in places, and streets and buildings stood on the resultant Quayside.

Strong defences were also constructed. Work on an imposing town wall started in, or shortly after, 1265 and progressed slowly. In fact, it was not until the early 15th century that the final section was built along the Quayside. The defences enclosed 150 acres (61ha).

Meanwhile, in line with events nationwide, from the mid 14th century the borough was badly affected

Part of the town wall near Westgate Road

by outbreaks of the Black Death. Consequently, by 1377 the population had fallen by around half from the figure at the start of the century, a downward trend that probably continued in subsequent decades.

A significant development occurred in May 1400. Henry IV granted the borough a charter that severed the town from Northumberland, and henceforth Newcastle had its own sheriff. On the other hand, the royal castle remained part of Northumberland.

The most well known Novocastrian of this era was Roger Thornton, Newcastle's 'Dick Whittington', a very wealthy merchant who played a prominent role in the town's affairs and served as mayor nine times. In addition, in the early 15th century he founded a hospital called the *Maison Dieu*. He did so in Sandhill, a neighbourhood on the riverfront just east of the Tyne

Bridge. The hospital, which adjoined the town's seat of government, the Guildhall, was constructed to house nine poor men and four poor women.

Overall, Newcastle's fortunes were at a low ebb in the 15th century. Matters finally began to improve in around 1470, and the Guildhall was rebuilt in 1509. On the other hand, unbeknown to anyone, the days of the town's religious houses, a nunnery dating from the 12th century and several friaries founded in the 13th, were drawing to a close. The end came in 1539-40 when they were shut by Henry VIII during the Dissolution of the Monasteries.

In 1549 economic activity at Newcastle reportedly included the 'making and mending' of ships. By this date, moreover, a grammar school likely existed in the town—the traditional date for its foundation is 1545. The school was located near St Nicholas Church, which had been almost entirely rebuilt in the 14th and 15th centuries and now boasted an eye-catching tower.

Shortly after the accession of Queen Elizabeth in 1558, the Anglican Church was established and so staunch Protestant clergy were appointed to serve in Newcastle. Most residents accepted the new state of affairs and the town remained loyal to the Crown in 1569 when the North East witnessed an unsuccessful Catholic rebellion, one of whose leaders was the Earl of Northumberland.

During the second half of the 16th century, coal shipments increased at a rapid pace and by the close of the century approximately 200,000 tons were being shipped annually. Although some of the coal went abroad, the main market was London. In March 1600, Elizabeth I granted the town's hostmen, so-called because their activities included hosting visiting merchants, a charter that established the Company of Hostmen and it was this company that dominated the Tyne's coal trade.

In 1636 Newcastle was hit extremely hard by an outbreak of plague that lasted several months and killed at least 5,600 of its inhabitants, approximately 47 per cent of the population. Not surprisingly, the most badly affected areas were poor neighbourhoods and especially Sandgate, located beside the river in the southeast corner of the town.

Further disruption was caused by the Civil War that started in 1642. Newcastle was held for Charles I. Parliament therefore imposed an embargo on the Tyne's coal trade. Moreover, in the late summer and autumn of 1644 Newcastle was besieged by a large Scottish army that had entered England to support the king's opponents. Finally, on 19 October, the Scots launched a full-scale assault and 'after two houres very hot dispute' began to enter the town, which was soon in their hands. Troops defending the castle held out for another three days before capitulating.

After the Civil War, parts of the town underwent significant rebuilding. In the late 1650s, for example, the Guildhall was rebuilt on a larger scale to a design by Robert Trollope.

As the century drew to a close, Newcastle was visited by an aristocratic traveller, Celia Fiennes. She did so in 1698 and was impressed by what she found. Among other things, she noted the presence of fine pleasure gardens and concluded that Newcastle was 'a noble town of great trade' and resembled London more than any other place in England. For his part, in the 1720s Daniel Defoe, likewise touring the country, described Newcastle as 'not the pleasantest place in the world to live in'. He was, though, impressed by the local shipbuilding industry (based on the riverside to the east of the town) and noted: 'They build Ships here to Perfection.'

For centuries, Newcastle's wealthiest inhabitants lived in the Close and Sandhill, districts located along the riverfront in the southwest quarter of the town. However, by Defoe's day the affluent were moving to dwellings located in the upper part of Newcastle.

Other noteworthy events of this era included the arrival of John Wesley in 1742—the visit led to the establishment of the region's first Methodist preaching house in Newcastle—and the founding of the infirmary in 1751. Moreover, arguably the first proper provincial bank in England opened in Pilgrim Street in 1755. In addition, a new Tyne Bridge was built after the medieval one was badly damaged by a flood in 1771, by which time the process of removing sections of the town wall had commenced.

In 1801 Newcastle's population numbered 33,000, which meant that demographic growth had not kept pace with some other major urban centres, a fact that was not well received by some of the town's proud inhabitants.

Under the Municipal Corporations Act of 1835, Newcastle was enlarged by the addition of neighbouring townships, including Elswick and Jesmond. By this date a major redevelopment programme had just started in the upper part of the town. The scheme, orchestrated by a wealthy building contractor named Richard Grainger, lasted six years and resulted in nine new streets—including Grey Street, complete with the imposing Theatre Royal—and the construction of Grainger Market. Interestingly, in 1838 Emerson Muschamp Bainbridge founded a drapery store near Grainger Market, and soon provided customers with a wide range of product lines. Arguably, in so doing he created the country's first department store.

Despite progress made, much still needed to be done to enhance living conditions in Newcastle. A report published in 1845 by a government inspector observed:

> In this populous city…parts of the borough…are in an extremely neglected condition, many new streets are unpaved and in a dangerous state; such house and private drains that exist in the houses of the middle and higher classes are generally defective and offensive, the dwellings of the poor are very deficient in all conveniences and necessaries…[and] there are large public depôts for refuse in objectionable places.

From the mid 19th century, Newcastle's residents could travel by rail—the first local line to operate was the Newcastle & Carlisle Railway in the second half of the 1830s. In the next decade, the High Level Bridge, a two-tier structure, whose upper level was built to carry trains, was constructed. The bridge was designed by the renowned local engineer, Robert Stephenson. In August 1850, moreover, Queen Victoria and Prince Albert came to Newcastle to open the impressive Central Station, designed by the region's leading architect, John Dobson.

A short distance to the east of the Central Station, stands Newcastle Cathedral. For centuries, this was simply the parish church of St Nicholas. In 1882, though, the church was elevated to cathedral status when Newcastle and Northumberland were severed from the historic bishopric of Durham to form a new diocese. Consequently, Newcastle gained city status.

By this date Newcastle's infrastructure included the Swing Bridge, which had opened in 1876 and replaced the bridge erected in the late 18th century. The new bridge enabled ships to travel further upstream than had been the case. The superstructure and hydraulic machinery of the crossing were manufactured at Elswick by the Tyne's leading engineering firm, a business founded in 1847 by William Armstrong and several partners; a firm that now added to its diverse operations there by starting to produce ships as well.

In their leisure moments, Armstrong's workforce and fellow residents of Newcastle were able to enjoy a wide range of recreational opportunities.

The Victorian Central Station

They could, for example, visit the Central Library that had opened in 1850 or stroll around Leazes Park, which opened in 1873. Various sporting activities were also available. Football, in particular, struck a chord and several clubs existed. In 1892 two of these merged to form Newcastle United Football Club, which was based at St James's Park and joined the Second Division of the Football League the following year. In the Edwardian era, the club was one of the best in England. The team were League Champions on three occasions and won the FA Cup in 1910.

Some fans travelled to matches by tram. These had begun to run in the late 1870s and were initially horse-powered. The year 1902 saw the introduction of electric trams, two years after an electric system had come into use at Sunderland, Newcastle's largest rival in the region.

Newcastle had over 215,000 inhabitants by 1901—the figure for Sunderland was 146,000—and the population soon grew significantly as a result of boundary changes. For instance, Walker, located just downstream and a major centre of shipbuilding, was one of several neighbouring communities that became part of the city in 1904. Newcastle's first council houses, mostly two-roomed dwellings, opened there in 1906.

The Edwardian era also witnessed the advent of cinemas. Although moving pictures had been shown at various venues in the city (the first were seen in 1896) Newcastle's first full-time cinema, the Star Hall, opened

Opposite: Grainger Street c.1900

Newcastle Cathedral viewed from near the castle, c.1888

in April 1908. The same year also saw the opening of six other cinemas in the city as well.

World War One, of course, had a profound impact. For one thing, the local economy experienced a dramatic rise in activity. This is illustrated by the fact that Armstrong Whitworth's, a firm based at Elswick and formed by merger in 1897, took on many workers to meet demand. The workforce almost trebled by the time the war ended in 1918. The firm's output included armaments produced at Elswick, aircraft constructed at Gosforth, and warships erected at its impressive Walker Naval Yard that had opened in 1913. In addition, other ships built at Walker were produced by Swan, Hunter & Wigham Richardson Ltd, a Tyneside firm formed by merger in 1903 and one of whose yards, the Neptune Yard, had been founded at Walker in 1860.

Following the war, increasing motor traffic led to the construction of the present Tyne Bridge in 1925-8. It was built to ease growing congestion at the nearby Swing Bridge and at the High Level Bridge.

A transformation in the city's housing stock occurred during the inter-war years. For one thing, 11,000 council houses were constructed in the period 1919-35. Moreover, semi-detached private homes were built

Opposite: The Tyne Bridge with the Millennium Bridge further downstream

in large numbers and were mostly intended to accommodate artisans and members of the lower-middle-class.

High levels of unemployment blighted many lives between the wars. Walker Naval Yard, for example, was almost permanently closed between 1928 and 1935. Furthermore, the period saw the decline in the importance of coal to Newcastle's economy. Walker Colliery closed in 1920. At another pit dating from the 18th century, Montagu Colliery in Scotswood, the number of employees fell significantly, from 1,265 in 1921, to 722 by 1940.

On the other hand, people in work enjoyed a rise in their spending power as prices fell faster than wages. Among new retail outlets that graced the city in this period was Marks and Spencer, whose branch in Northumberland Street opened in 1932. Well-established businesses included Bainbridge's, and another major department store, Fenwick's, the latter dating from 1882. Such shops were significant sources of female employment.

The inter-war years also experienced a marked rise in popularity for cinemas and 27 opened in the city, particularly in the 1930s. The most notable was the Paramount. It could seat 2,602 patrons and opened in Pilgrim Street in 1931. Of the plush cinema, Frank Manders aptly comments: 'the Paramount was undoubtedly the city's premier cinema and a visit to it was a special event.' Other new venues included the Apollo Cinema on Shields Road in Byker, which opened in 1933 but was destroyed by a bomb early on 6 May 1941. It was the city's only cinema to be closed by enemy action. Fortunately, Newcastle was not as heavily bombed as some of the country's other major towns and cities during World War Two. For example, civilian deaths in the city numbered 141, less than at the boroughs of South Shields, Tynemouth, and Sunderland, the last of which had the highest number of civilian fatalities in the region, 267.

Some of the aircraft that defended the North East were based at Woolsington where a modest civil airstrip had opened in 1935. Civilian use recommenced in the late 1940s and the site has since developed into Newcastle International Airport.

One of the major facets of the history of post-war Newcastle is the decline of traditional industries. Coal's importance continued its downward course. Indeed, in 1947 when coal mines were nationalised, Montagu was the only colliery operating within the city's boundaries and its days were numbered. Closure followed in 1959. Overall, shipbuilding likewise fared badly, partly due to growing competition from yards in the Far East. In the late 1960s Newcastle's shipyards became part of Tyneside's Swan Hunter Group, which thereafter operated three yards on the north side of the river. These included the Naval Yard and Neptune Yard at Walker. Nationalisation followed in 1977 and both yards closed during the following decade.

Turning to other matters, 1958 saw the start of construction work on the Civic Centre near Haymarket, a project that was completed in 1969. Of the eye-catching complex, Thomas Faulkner aptly notes: 'Certainly, the Civic Centre cannot be accused of failing to make a grand statement.'

During the 1960s, as part of a process of redevelopment, the city centre underwent large-scale demolition that included the loss of buildings of historic and architectural value. Among other things, most of Eldon Square (erected in the years 1825-31) was pulled down to make way for the vast indoor Eldon Square Shopping Centre. Queen Elizabeth II performed the official opening ceremony in 1977 and the centre remains a vibrant part of Newcastle's retail sector. One of the shops that had relocated to the centre in 1976 was Bainbridge's, which became John Lewis in 2002.

The 1960s redevelopment programme also resulted in the construction of unappealing high-rise blocks of flats, and radical changes to the road network. Slum clearance also occurred in peripheral areas such as Scotswood and Walker. Major demolition happened in order to improve housing standards in overcrowded areas, a process that entailed moving some residents to new homes elsewhere, many of which were located outside the boundaries of the city, at, for example, Killingworth; a situation that contributed to Newcastle's late 20th century population decline.

The city has two major centres of higher learning, namely the University of Northum-

The Civic Centre

bria, a former polytechnic founded in 1968 that was granted university status in 1992; and Newcastle University. The latter traces its roots to a College of Medicine and a College of Physical Science founded in the 19th century. In the 1930s the colleges, both outlying parts of the University of Durham, merged to become King's College. Thereafter, in 1963 the connection with Durham ceased when the college became the University of Newcastle upon Tyne.

Since the 1980s, the Quayside— which had become a rather neglected area—has been regener-

St James's Park viewed from
Newcastle's Chinatown

ated to become a lively part of Newcastle's recreational life, as is attested by numerous bars and clubs. As Natasha Vall comments: 'By the 1990s, the economy of urban sociability dominated the Quayside area and little remained of the river's earlier commercial functions.'

Only one of the cinemas founded in Newcastle during the 20th century is still in business, namely the independent Tyneside Cinema on Pilgrim Street, a venue that first opened in 1937 (under a different name) and was restored and enlarged in 2006-8. Meanwhile, at the end of 2002 the Odeon, a multiplex cinema with 12 screens and 2,569 seats, had opened in the Gate complex on Newgate Street.

Whereas the popularity of cinemas waned significantly in the post-war decades, football remained of vital importance to many of the city's inhabitants and continues to do so. Newcastle United has generally ranked among the top flight of the nation's clubs, and enjoyed a golden period in the 1950s. So much so, that the club won the FA Cup on three occasions, namely in 1951, 1952 and 1955. The star player of the era was Jackie Milburn. 'Wor Jackie', as he was affectionately known, had signed for the club in 1943 and remained with Newcastle until his retirement in 1957, by which time his tally of goals for Newcastle numbered 200, a record only exceeded by Alan Shearer, who was born in Newcastle in 1970. In the closing years of the 20th century, St James's Park was transformed. By 2000 the ground had become an impressive stadium capable of seating over 52,000 fans. Several matches were played at the ground as part of the 2012 Olympics, thereby enhancing the city's international profile.

Newcastle's population numbers around 279,000, and the city is undoubtedly the capital of the North East.

NORTHUMBERLAND'S DESPERADOES,
the Story of the Border Reivers

For James Dodd of Burnmouth it was the end of the line. The year 1523 was drawing to a close and Jamie, described by an officer of the Crown as 'the most named thief of all others,' was about to end his days with a noose around his neck.

James came from near Tarset in a tributary valley of the North Tyne and was a member of a lawless society—the Border Reivers—that had developed in the western uplands of Northumberland, especially North Tynedale and Redesdale. News of the criminality of the reivers (a name derived from their practice of stealing livestock) reached the highest levels of society. For instance, only a few months before Jamie's execution, the Earl of Surrey noted that Henry VIII was 'marvellous discontended with the robberies and murders committed by the men of Tynedale and Redesdale.'

Earlier still, in 1498 Richard Fox, the Bishop of Durham, had admonished the inhabitants of both dales, which lay in his vast diocese, for their waywardness. The valleys, he said, were infested with 'infamous robbers' steeped in lives of crime—villainous rogues who boasted of their deeds in taverns and elsewhere and taught their children to regard theft as an art.

Essentially, this state of affairs had developed in the late Middle Ages when, partly as a result of the Anglo-Scottish wars, legitimate public authority became increasingly ineffectual in the districts in question. Hence by the beginning of the Tudor period in 1485, the dales had a well-established reputation for lawbreaking.

In North Tyndale, the Charltons were the most prominent of the clans or 'surnames'. Other significant kinship groups were the Robsons, Dodds (also Dodd) and Milburns. In the words of the historian Ralph Robson, Bellingham, the location of a Saturday market and an annual fair, 'was the capital of their Lilliputian realm where they not only purchased bread, ale and other provisions' but assembled whenever they had matters to discuss among themselves. In neighbouring Redesdale, on the other hand, the most notable surnames were Hall, Reed, Hedley, Fletcher and Potts.

Reivers lived in scattered farmsteads or hamlets, and in some instances the residents did not all belong to the same surname. However, temporary settlements—shielings—were occupied on the high moorland between April and August when livestock was grazed on the extensive moors and each shieling was exclusive to members of a particular clan.

Of course, in addition to farming, members of these communities (some of whom, owing to over-population, lived on meagre holdings that enhanced the appeal of a life of crime), supported themselves by stealing livestock, extorting protection money and kidnapping. In their criminal ventures— which sometimes included homicide—members of one surname often acted in concert with reivers from one or more of the others. In addition, there were strong links between the dales, as well as cross-border family ties.

The main raiding season lasted from October to February, although there was a lull in the depths of winter. Mounted reivers usually rode tough, unshod ponies, and wore steel bonnets (helmets that normally left the face exposed) and padded jackets that could be iron-plated. Furthermore, most had leather boots that reached to the thigh. The standard weapon was the lance, but swords and bows were also used. So, too, were firearms, and as the 16th century drew to a close some reivers brandished pairs of pistols.

The majority of raids occurred in the upland zone. Reivers frequently crossed into Scotland, on occasion with the support of the Crown, to prey on other clan-based groups like the Armstrongs and Elliotts who answered in kind. The reivers also turned their unwelcome attention to the more civilised parts of Northumberland and neighbouring counties.

Sometimes the dales were raided by the authorities in an attempt to assert control. In 1526 for example, 16 reivers, mostly from Redesdale, were executed at a particularly thorough assize. But bringing reivers to justice was seldom easy. For one thing, the reivers operated a good intelligence network within the dales. In addition, witnesses were often intimidated, making it difficult to secure convictions.

In North Tynedale, a notable example of lawlessness briefly centred around a figure named Will Ridley. He was sent into the valley in the autumn of 1523 by his kinsman, Sir Nicholas Ridley of Willimoteswick, to cause trouble for officers of the Crown with whom Sir Nicholas was at odds. Will soon amassed a strong force of around 400 followers, a number of whom came from Redesdale. The man responsible for policing the dale was Sir Ralph Fenwick, who was based at Tarset Castle. However, in November he was forced to flee at the head of 80 horsemen when he was opposed by a superior force under one of Ridley's henchmen who 'set upon the said Sir Rauff…and chased the said Sir Rauff out of Tyndaill.'

Subsequently, during 1525 Will and his men plundered widely over Northumberland and County Durham. In North Tynedale itself, a royal garrison of mounted archers at Tarset was attacked twice and the second assault witnessed the killing of female camp followers as well as soldiers. But shortly thereafter, the government tightened its grip and as Robson's notes, Ridley 'vanished like a wraith.'

Nevertheless, in future years, reivers remained troublesome. There fore, in April 1528 six hostages who had been handed over to ensure good behaviour were hanged by the Earl of Northumberland at Morpeth, owing to the failure of fellow clansmen to behave as the earl desired. Moreover, in December 1538 reivers descended on Hexham, where some North Tynedalers were incarcerated in Hexham Gaol, and forcibly freed them.

Hexham Gaol

In the second half of the century Bernard Gilpin, the Rector of Houghton-le-Spring in County Durham, made a valiant effort to improve conditions in the dales. Gilpin, the 'Apostle of the North', undertook annual visits to North Tynedale and Redesdale and to some extent mitigated the criminality that was their hallmark.

His desire to preach there was certainly not universally shared. In 1596, for example, a certain 'Mr Crackenthorpe, Master of Arts at Oxford…a devout and godly and learned man', declined the living of Simonburn in North Tynedale, 'deeming his body unable to live in so troublesome a place and his nature not well brooking the perverse nature of so crooked a people.'

For much of the reiving period, buildings in the dales were mostly of timber construction. However, during the 16th century the bastle became the characteristic dwelling in the area—the first such were erected in around the 1540s. Although these fortified homes were most numerous in the haunts of the reivers, they were also built elsewhere in the region in a swathe of country extending roughly 20 miles (32km) in depth from the line of the border.

A bastle was a small stone farmhouse, invariably rectangular in plan, with walls approximately 4ft (1.2m) thick and a steeply pitched gable roof covered with slate. There was a byre on the ground floor and living space for the family on an upper floor. Access to the family's living area was through an upper door, reached via a retractable ladder, in one of the side walls, but stone stairways were later provided instead.

The most well known bastle is Black Middens, which lies in the upper reaches of Tarsetdale in North Tynedale, and in 1583 it was one of eight homesteads in the valley attacked by around 300 Armstrongs under a laird named Will Armstrong of Kinmont, whose raid included the killing of six people. Of events, we read:

> On frydaie in the mornynge last, being the xxxth of August, in Tynedale unto certin places, that is to say the Keyne, the Reidheughe, the Black Myddynes, the Hill Howse, the Water head, the Starr head, and the Bog head, the High Feelde, [Armstrong and his men] there raysed fyer and brunt the most parte of them, and…stale and drave away fowre hundrethe sheip and goate, and XXX horses and mears…and slewe and murdered crewellie six parsons, and maimed and hurte ellevin parsons, and took and led away XXX prisoners.

Opposite: Black Middens bastle

Certainly, Scottish reivers, who sometimes numbered several thousand, repeatedly inflicted misery in Redesdale and North Tynedale in the closing decades of the century. In addition to driving off livestock, the Scots dealt out further death and destruction. For example, of eight Dodds and two Robsons slain in early 1597, three were youngsters burned alive in their homes.

Growing poverty was a feature of life in Northumberland during the last third of the 16th century, and both dales were undoubtedly affected. In 1595 this point was noted by a government officer, Lord Eure. At a muster of men from the valleys—noted only a few decades earlier for producing accomplished light horsemen, albeit of course best known for reiving— Eure lamented that the practice of dividing land holdings between sons had contributed to a situation in which the men who assembled were undernourished and poorly equipped. Indeed, very few possessed mounts.

In such circumstances, both dales became increasingly impoverished. In 1597, for example, Eure described Redesdale as a 'miserable, distressed and wretched country.' Hence the valleys witnessed a decline in population, partly owing to migration to less fraught surroundings and some of those who left went to work in Tyneside's rapidly expanding coal industry. The heyday of the Border Reivers was over.

'PETRIFIED WITH FEAR',
WILLIAM WALLACE & NORTHUMBERLAND

I t was autumn, 1297, and news from Scotland—bad news—had arrived in Northumberland. It was sweeping through the county like wildfire, causing fear and alarm as it did so. An English army campaigning in Scotland, and within whose ranks were men drawn from Northumberland, had come to grief at Stirling Bridge on 11 September, having been crushingly defeated by a Scottish army determined to drive the English out of Scotland, an army that would now very likely follow up its victory by striking into England itself.

Understandably, Northumberland's inhabitants felt more vulnerable than most. Not for nothing did the chronicler Walter of Guisborough state, 'the Northumbrians were petrified with fear, and they evacuated from the countryside their wives and children and all their household goods, sending them with their animals to Newcastle and various other places throughout the provinces.'

The train of events that led to Anglo-Scottish conflict in the late 13th century began in 1286 when Scotland's king, Alexander III, died after falling from his horse, leaving his young granddaughter, Margaret, as the rightful heir to the Scottish throne. In 1290 an agreement was ratified whereby she would marry the heir of England's king, Edward I, but that autumn Margaret followed her grandfather to the grave and the royal line of Scotland failed.

Thirteen claimants to the throne came forward and overtures were made to Edward requesting his involvement in the proceedings so that the succession could be determined without recourse to civil war. On 17 November 1292, Edward, who regarded himself as the overlord of Scotland and was accepted as such by the claimants, chose one of them, John Balliol, to be the new king and subsequently received his homage at Newcastle while spending Christmas on Tyneside.

In mid 1295, however, the Scottish parliament wrested power from Balliol and vested it in a council which proceeded to ratify an alliance with the French—with whom Edward had been at war since 1294—promising mutual support if needed.

An English invasion of Scotland ensued in March 1296. The campaign resulted in the capture and sacking of Berwick upon Tweed by English troops on 30 March, the defeat of a Scottish force at Dunbar, and Balliol's subsequent surrender and abdication in the summer. Edward then held a parliament at Berwick where he received the homage of many important Scots. He then returned to England leaving the governance of Scotland to trusted English lieutenants.

But in 1297 events took a dramatic turn—widespread rebellion broke out. One of the leaders of opposition to English rule was a man of knightly family, though not himself a knight, none other than William Wallace, who has been dramatically portrayed by Mel Gibson in the blockbusting film, *Braveheart,* an action-packed epic that pays little attention to historical reality. Born near Paisley in around 1272, Wallace killed the sheriff of Lanark in May 1297, thereby triggering off the first of the risings in Scotland that year which developed into full-scale rebellion.

To counter the unrest, an English army advanced from Berwick to Stirling, where combined rebel forces had gathered under the leadership of Wallace and the aristocratic Andrew Murray. Hence, as mentioned above, battle was joined on 11 September and the English were routed. One of the Englishmen who perished was Hugh de Cressingham, a hated official, whose corpse was skinned by the exultant victors and some of the skin was reportedly used to make a sword-belt for Wallace.

What is certain is that the defeat sent shock waves through the northern counties of England—the Scots would very likely follow up their victory by striking across the border! After all, had not cross border raids occurred the previous year? Indeed they had. At Hexham, for instance, the Scots had driven away the Augustinian canons of Hexham Priory—a religious house founded in the early 12th century—and had plundered the monastery and set both it and the town alight. History, it seemed, was about to repeat itself.

A statue of William Wallace

The Scots duly retook the town of Berwick (but not the castle) and likely did so before 11 October. In the same month marauding bands struck deep into Northumberland. For instance Felton mill on the River Coquet was burnt by Scots on about 13 October, the earliest datable destruction wrought in the wake of Stirling Bridge in the county. The only resistance to the raiders is said to have been offered by castle garrisons, such as that of Alnwick.

At the beginning of November Wallace himself appeared on the scene

St Wilfrid's Gate – the main gatehouse at Hexham Priory

with his army and things took an altogether more serious turn. The *Lanercost Chronicle*—written in Cumbria—sadly summarized events as follows: 'The Scots gathered together and invaded, devastating the whole country, causing burnings, depredations and murders, and they came almost up to the town of Newcastle, but turned away from it and invaded the county of Carlisle … and afterwards they returned to Northumberland, to devastate more fully anything they had overlooked previously.'

During the initial invasion Wallace advanced into Tynedale—he made no attempt to take Newcastle—where his forces did a great deal of damage at Bywell before pressing on and burning Corbridge, the second most important borough in Northumberland and a place that had suffered from Scottish aggression the previous year. Wallace then advanced further along the valley of the Tyne. His destination?—Hexham. Here, on 7 November, he granted the priory a letter of protection, no doubt after the canons had agreed to pay protection money.

Wallace duly advanced westward on Carlisle, whose defences he did not attempt to storm. Then, after ravaging much of Cumbria and having been reinforced, he retraced his steps and marched back into Tynedale. At Hexham he found only three canons still remaining. He demanded to hear Mass and then left the church to discard his weapons before returning for the service. While he was away, some of his men stole the chalice and other sacred altar vessels. Hearing this, an angry and embar-

Opposite: Mitford Castle

rassed Wallace demanded to know who had committed the sacrilege but to no avail, whereupon he confessed to the canons that those who had perpetrated the deed were rough, uncivilized men, who had no shame.

Wallace remained at Hexham Priory for two days, using it as a base from which the surrounding countryside could be raided. Upon leaving, he headed further down the valley of the Tyne during bitter weather. He destroyed Wylam en route towards the partially fortified town of Newcastle (where town walls had been commenced years earlier but were still not complete) and whose castle garrison comprised six men-at-arms, 60 crossbowmen and 40 other archers.

But as was the case with Carlisle, Wallace did not attempt to storm the town. According to Walter of Guisborough, 'the courageous men who were in charge of Newcastle braced themselves and went out of the city a little way, despite the fact that they were very few against many. Seeing this, the Scots veered away from the city, divided among themselves the spoils [and] departed to their own regions.' While they were homeward bound, the castle at Mitford, beside the River Wansbeck near Morpeth, was attacked and largely destroyed on 25 November.

Edward I retaliated the following year and inflicted a major defeat on Wallace at Falkirk on 22 July, a battle in which men from the North East once again participated. Resistance continued, nevertheless. Indeed, Wallace remained a thorn in Edward's side as a guerrilla leader until his capture and barbarous execution in 1305, by which date Scotland had to all intents and purposes been conquered, albeit briefly —Robert the Bruce was waiting in the wings, soon to rekindle Scottish nationalism, with disastrous consequences once again for the people of Northumberland.

STEAM & SPEED,
THE STEPHENSONS & THEIR EXPLOITS

W hen the Scottish publisher William Chambers arrived in Newcastle in late 1949 (en route to preside at a meeting of Sunderland's Literary and Philosophical Society) he was eager to explore the region's capital.

In particular, he was enthralled by the High Level Bridge erected in the years 1845-9. It was a two-tier structure—the upper level was built to carry trains—that spanned the Tyne between Newcastle and Gateshead and was designed by a man of local origin, Robert Stephenson, the renowned son of the famous pioneering figure in railway history, George Stephenson.

In a fascinating account of his visit (published in *Chambers' Edinburgh Review*), William Chambers notes that the bridge contained 'six arches of open iron-work, which, seen at a distance, appear like a stripe of lace drawn across the sky....The piers of the arches are of stone—light, elegant stalks planted in the bottom of the river.'

Chambers was given a guided tour of the structure and recorded: 'I had the pleasure of walking along the upper bridge and being conducted through the lower by the assistant-engineer, Mr R. Hodgson, who explained a number of the details....While we walked...a railway train went overhead roaring like a peal of thunder; and the only thing to be feared is, that the noise of the trains may startle horses.'

Chambers also tells us that before 'the bridge was opened for trains it was exposed to a severe test. Four of the heaviest locomotives were yoked together, and driven backwards and forwards for upwards of an hour; and scarcely anything is more indicative of high engineering skill than the fact, that at this vast trial of its powers of endurance the structure did not show the slightest symptom of weakness or vibration.'

Newcastle's impressive new bridge was part of a remarkable process that was transforming the region's infrastructure and Robert Stephenson was at the forefront of technological developments.

This had of course also been true of his father, George, who was born into humble circumstances at a cottage just to the east of Wylam in the Tyne valley in 1781. Owing to his low birth, George was largely self-taught and, in the words of Richard Lomas had 'an inborn ability to identify a problem and then to work out how it could be solved, qualities supported by ambition, boundless self-confidence, determination and perseverance.'

George worked at a number of Tyneside collieries from his youth onward in various capacities. Among the pits in question was one at Willington Quay (where his son Robert was born in 1803) and another at Killing-

George Stephenson's birthplace at Wylam

worth. However, following the death of his wife in 1806, George left the latter mine and spent two years north of the border. He then returned to Killingworth where, owing to his ability, he was subsequently placed in charge of all the steam engines (used for extracting water and coal) at that colliery and others owned by the same consortium. Moreover, in 1813-4 Stephenson built his first steam-powered locomotive for Killingworth's wagonway, part of a well-established network of horse-powered wagonways along which coal was conveyed from collieries to the Tyne.

George Stephenson was, however, not the only Tynesider interested in using steam power, instead of horses, to haul coal by rail. Other pioneering figures included William Hedley—born at Newburn on Tyne in 1779—and Timothy Hackworth who came into the world at Wylam in 1786.

While working at Wylam Colliery, Hedley and Hackworth collaborated to design steam-powered locomotives that commenced operating in 1814 and hauled coal to Lemington-on-Tyne. One of their engines was none other than *Puffing Billy*, which remained in use until 1862 and is now on display in the Science Museum in London.

Furthermore, by the summer of 1815 other collieries at Kenton, Coxlodge, Heaton and Wallsend had also acquired locomotives and Tyneside was well and truly at the forefront of railway development.

Not surprisingly, the introduction of locomotives was not trouble free. At Wallsend in 1815, for example, trials of the *Steam Elephant*—designed by William Chapman, a Yorkshire-born engineer based in Newcastle—ended in disappointment for the wooden rails of the wagonway were unsatisfactory. The *Steam Elephant* was thus subsequently mothballed until an iron track was laid a few years later. Of developments in general, Andy Guy comments that the 'locomotive entered 1816 battered but still breathing.' Indeed, although progress of course continued to be made, it was not until the 1830s that the general adoption of locomotive power commenced.

In the interim, George Stephenson had been employed to design a railway in County Durham for businessmen sinking Hetton Colliery, the first pit to be sunk through magnesian limestone covering much of the coalfield in the north-eastern part of that county. Stephenson was given the task of designing a line that would link the pit (which opened in 1822) to staithes at Sunderland. Interestingly, the railway that resulted was the first complete line to be engineered by Wylam's most famous son and crossed undulating terrain on its eight-mile route to Sunderland. Hence it was a hybrid line. Coal was not only hauled along the rails by locomotives built by Stephenson, but was also drawn along the line by stationary steam engines. Where gradients were favourable, self-acting inclines were also part of the scheme.

George Stephenson

Shortly thereafter, George designed the world's first public railway (likewise in County Durham) namely the Stockton and Darlington Railway which opened in 1825. In addition to passengers, the line was also built to carry coal to the port of Stockton-on-Tees. For the first stage of the journey, haulage was provided by stationary engines but locomotive-power was employed from the vicinity of West Auckland onward.

Locomotives used on the Stockton and Darlington Railway, including the celebrated *Locomotion*, were manufactured on Tyneside at the recently established engine works of Robert Stephenson and Co. located at Forth Street in Newcastle, a firm run by George's talented young son who, thanks to his father, had received a good formal education. Robert had attended one of the region's leading private schools, Dr Bruce's Academy in Percy Street, Newcastle, and had also gone to Edinburgh University, albeit for only six months.

George Stephenson ranked among the partners in his son's firm. This was also true of Michael Longridge, the owner of the Bedlington Ironworks, which had produced parts, such as axles and boilerplates, for George Stephenson's first locomotive in 1814 and whose output included rails for the Stockton and Darlington Railway. Shortly after the Forth Street plant opened, Robert Stephenson headed off to work in South America and Longridge thus managed the factory in his absence.

Robert was abroad from 1824 until 1827, when he returned to England and promptly joined his father who was designing the Liverpool and Manchester Railway, which opened in 1830. During this period, Robert also undertook locomotive development at the Forth Street Works where the famous *Rocket*, whose maximum speed was 35 miles an hour, was built in 1829. It was the world's most advanced locomotive and the lion's share

Opposite: Robert Stephenson's High Level Bridge at Newcastle viewed from upstream

of the credit for its design probably belongs to Robert, although his father was also involved.

In subsequent years, George Stephenson's activity was largely confined to the Midlands where he died near Chesterfield in 1848. On the other hand, Robert's reputation went from strength to strength and he became a celebrated railway engineer. Indeed, such was his international reputation that he was involved in projects as far afield as Canada, Egypt, Norway and India.

As noted above, Robert was also responsible for designing Newcastle's High Level Bridge. In 1844 Tyneside had been linked to London by rail, but the northern section of the line terminated at Gateshead. However, Newcastle Corporation was eager to have the region's main station within its own boundaries. Hence it played a key role in developments that led to the construction of the High Level Bridge. This was built to carry the line across the Tyne to an impressive station designed by the region's foremost architect, John Dobson, who had been born at North Shields in 1787. Newcastle Central Station was officially opened by Queen Victoria in August 1850.

Moreover, from Tyneside a journey could be continued northward by means of the Newcastle to Berwick Railway, which was designed by the Stephensons and laid in the years 1844-7. Robert then proceeded to design the imposing Royal Border Bridge which carried the railway across the Tweed at Berwick (it replaced a temporary wooden viaduct) and the impressive new bridge was likewise opened by Queen Victoria and Prince Albert in August 1850.

By this date Robert Stephenson's outstanding career was drawing to an end. He died at his house in London in 1859 and was held in such high regard that he was interred at Westminster Abbey. Like his father, he is rightly remembered as one of Tyneside's greatest sons.

THE FARNE ISLANDS

The Farne Islands lie some two to five miles (3.2 to 8km) off the coast of Northumberland—the closest place on the mainland is Bamburgh—and are famous for their wildlife and links with notable figures in the early history of Northumbrian Christianity, especially St Cuthbert.

The Farnes are divided into inner and outer groups of islands and most of these are very small and comprise bare rock that disappears from view at high tide.

Among those that are permanent is Inner Farne, the largest of the islands, whose highest point is 62ft (19m) above mean sea level. The island is partly covered by grass and was the location of the hermitage of St Cuthbert, a former Bishop of Lindisfarne, who died here in 687. Bede describes the island as lying 'a few miles to the southeast of Lindisfarne, cut off on the landward side by very deep water and facing, on the other side, out toward the limitless ocean.'

In the Middle Ages, owing to Inner Farne's association with St Cuthbert, Durham Cathedral Priory established a cell on the island and manned it with a couple of monks sent from Durham. This event occurred in 1246 and the cell lasted until the Dissolution of the Monasteries in the late 1530s.

Over the centuries several beacons and lighthouses have been erected on the Farne Islands. The most famous is Longstone Lighthouse, built in 1825-6 by Trinity House at the furthest point of the outer group of islands. The lighthouse, like all in the UK since 1998, is now automatic but for most of its existence it was manned. The most well known keeper was William Darling, a figure thrust into the limelight in late 1838. On 7 September of that

year, he and his 22-year-old daughter Grace, boldly rescued nine survivors of a vessel, the *Forfarshire*,
that had struck one of the nearby
islands. The event attracted huge
publicity and thrust the pair, and
Grace in particular, into the realms
of celebrity.

In 1925 the Farne Islands were
sold to the National Trust by Lord
Armstrong. They attract numerous
visitors—regular boat trips are run
to the islands from Seahouses on
the mainland—and have become
popular for scuba diving and their
wildlife. The Farnes are home to a
colony of some five to six thousand
grey seals. Moreover, during the
breeding season the islands attract
approximately 100,000 birds. Puffins are most numerous. Other birds
that breed in large numbers include
arctic terns, black-legged kittiwakes,
common eider and shags.

Opposite: Longstone Lighthouse
Right: A pair of puffins and a curious seal
Below: Looking back towards the mainland

'THE FLOWERS OF THE FOREST',
James IV's Campaigns in Northumberland

A ccording to Don Pedro de Ayala, Spain's ambassador to Scotland in 1496-7, the king was 'of noble stature, neither tall nor short, and as handsome in complexion and shape as a man can be.' Of whom was he speaking? None other than James IV, a popular and able monarch who had ascended Scotland's throne in 1488 when aged 15. De Ayala was not the only person to write well of James. The noted scholar, Erasmus, declared that the king 'had a wonderful intellectual power, an astonishing knowledge of everything; an unconquerable magnanimity, and the most abundant generosity.'

James was adventurous and high-spirited, a man whose passions included hunting, hawking and womanizing. He was also a martial figure—de Ayala declared that the king did 'not think it right to begin any warlike undertaking without being himself the first in danger.' Hence his reign witnessed Anglo-Scottish conflict, for James invaded Northumberland more than once.

He first did so in 1496 when Henry VII was on England's throne. James invaded in support of a claimant to the English crown named Perkin Warbeck, the 'Duke of York.' His support for Warbeck was conditional. He had come to an agreement with him concerning Berwick upon Tweed. In 1482 Berwick had been captured by the English during the reign of James IV's father, and James made Warbeck agree that he would hand the town and castle of Berwick over to the Scots if he succeeded in gaining England's throne.

On 20 September 1496, James and Perkin crossed the Tweed into England near Coldstream and one of those also present was de Ayala. Heralds had been sent ahead to announce that no harm would be done to anyone who did allegiance to Warbeck. If James had hoped that the local populace would flock to join Perkin he was wrong. Instead, they fled with their livestock to the castles and towers guarding the valley of the River Till. For some, flight was in vain. The Scots attacked and destroyed strongholds at Tilmouth, Twizel and Duddo, slaying the occupants and seizing their sheep and cattle in the process. According to Polydore Vergil, (whom Henry VII asked to write a history of England), Warbeck was unsettled by the slaughter and implored James to spare his 'subjects', whereupon James is said to have retorted, 'you have called...the English your subjects, yet not one of them has offered to help in a war waged on your behalf.'

Perkin Warbeck soon returned to Scotland, but James and his men remained in Northumberland and besieged Heton Castle. On 25 September an attempt was made to undermine a section of the walling. But news that an English army was advancing from Newcastle arrived and transformed

Opposite: Norham Castle

the situation. James decided that enough was enough and promptly led his army back into Scotland.

For his part, in October Henry VII declared that as a result of James' short-lived invasion, war with Scotland was now 'open and at large' and urged his subjects to do everything they could on land and sea to harm the Scots. James expected the English to retaliate with an invasion of their own and took steps to strengthen his border defences, but no such assault came. Henry was distracted by internal unrest.

Instead, in the summer of 1497 history repeated itself when James invaded England again, although this time he did so unaccompanied by Warbeck who had just left Scotland. James' objective was Norham Castle, a border stronghold occupying a strategic position on the River Tweed. The castle had been founded in the early 12th century by a Bishop of Durham and belonged to one of his successors, Bishop Fox, of whom Francis Bacon observed: 'Foxe, Bishop of Durseme, a wise man, and one that could see through the present to the future… [had] caused his castle of Norham to be strongly fortified… and [had] manned it likewise with a very great number of tall soldiers.' By early August, Scottish artillery—including the famous cannon named Mons Meg—was thundering shot against the defences, within which Fox himself was present. Furthermore, Scottish soldiers were ravaging the neighbourhood. James directed the siege during daylight hours and spent the evenings playing cards with de Ayala.

Yet again, events did not go the king's way. Norham's garrison, led by its captain, Thomas Garth, offered stubborn resistance and refused to yield. Moreover, word arrived that a powerful English force under a tough soldier, the Earl of Surrey, was marching to Norham's relief. James thus decided to withdraw and recrossed the Tweed. For his part, Surrey likewise crossed the border—he did so on 15 August—and attacked castles and towers in the vicinity of Berwick. In response, James sent heralds to Surrey, suggesting that the future of Berwick itself should be determined either by a general engagement between their armies or by personal combat on the part of James and the earl.

Surrey therefore began preparing for battle. But no engagement occurred. James 'ffled shameffully and sodeynly with all his company', perhaps having reflected on the fact that Scottish armies, despite their bravery, usually came off worst in battles against the English. Surrey's army, 'vexid grevously all the tyme with contynuell Rayn and cold wedyr', therefore soon withdrew to Berwick.

Friendly relations between Scotland and England were subsequently established. Indeed, a Treaty of Perpetual Peace was concluded in 1502, and in the following year James married Henry VII's daughter, Margaret Tudor, who travelled north via Newcastle and Berwick. But in 1511, by which time James' brother-in-law Henry VIII had ascended England's throne, relations turned sour, especially after Henry joined a formidable coalition—the Holy League—ranged against Louis XII of France, the monarch of a land with which Scotland had had friendly relations for generations.

In the summer of 1513, Henry crossed the Channel to wage war in France. In response, James invaded England in late August, thereby honouring a promise to the French king that he would do so if Henry moved against Louis.

James crossed the Tweed at, or near, Coldstream with a formidable army and an impressive artillery train drawn by 400 oxen. He then moved downstream and besieged Norham Castle, whose walls were battered by his guns and whose garrison soon surrendered. James then headed south. He captured another stronghold, Etal, and received the capitulation of nearby Ford Castle.

Henry VIII had entrusted the defence of England to the elderly Earl of Surrey. In early September, the earl arrived on the scene, intent on bringing the Scots to battle. He did just that on the inclement afternoon of 9 September, not far from Coldstream. Although Surrey was evidently outnumbered at the Battle of Flodden, he emerged victorious. It soon became apparent that the Scots' principal weapon, 18ft-long Swiss pikes, were not as effective as the bills—weapons resembling agricultural scythes—used by many English troops. The tips of the pikes were chopped off and when the Scots used their secondary weapons such as swords, they found themselves again at a disadvantage for they were outreached by their assailants. Not for nothing did Bishop Ruthal of Durham (who was not present) subsequently write: 'Our bills...did more goode that day thenne bowes for they shortely disapointed the Scotes of their long speres wherin was their greatest truste and whennne they came to hande strocke...they coude not resiste the billes that lighted so thicke and sore upon thaym.'

At some point, perhaps quite soon in the bloodbath, King James himself was cut down. According to a contemporary source, the *Articles of Battle*, he got to within a spear's length of Surrey when he fell, struck by an arrow and gashed by a bill. Many other high ranking Scots died. They included

A dramatic depiction of the Battle of Flodden

nine earls and the young Archbishop of St Andrew's (James' illegitimate son), who is said to have been so short-sighted that he 'could not read without holding his book to the very end of his nose.' The most moderate contemporary estimate of total Scottish losses was 5,000. Not surprisingly, Flodden ingrained itself on the Scottish national psyche and the battle is commemorated by the haunting pipe lament: 'The Flowers of the Forest are a 'wede away.'

TYNESIDE IN THE 1720s,
HISTORIC BUILDINGS & INDUSTRIAL ACTIVITY

In late April 1724 a Scotsman named Sir John Clerk of Penicuik crossed the border into England with one of his sons and two friends, and headed towards Newcastle upon Tyne. En route, they passed through Wooler, 'a small market town' in the foothills of the Cheviots, and spent the night at Morpeth's posthouse where they 'had excellent entertainment.'

Upon arrival at Newcastle on the 23rd, they lodged at the Black Bull Inn near the Town Hall and, after dining, set out to explore their surroundings. In particular they wished to see the Newcastle home of a prominent figure in the town's political and commercial life, Sir William Blackett, whose family had acquired a fortune through ventures such as mining and shipping. Sir William, who had represented Newcastle in parliament since 1710, was in his thirties and his possessions also included the Wallington estate in Northumberland where, much to the disappointment of the rebels who had counted on his support, he had gone into hiding in 1715 during the unsuccessful Jacobite rebellion intended to restore the exiled House of Stuart to the throne.

Of Blackett's home on Tyneside, Clerk notes: 'This Gentleman's predecessors gained a great Estate in Newcastle and built this house which is indeed something magnificent for a private man.' The Scot was not altogether impressed, however. 'The rooms are large but the Architecture in general is but confused.' He then notes the extensive grounds: 'The Gardens and park take up much Ground all within the walls of the city. The planting looks well but the fruit trees do not bear. The whole is kept in good order.'

From Blackett's imposing Newcastle residence (which was demolished in 1830), Sir John made his way down to the Tyne. The river, needless to say, was throbbing with activity. It had 'the appearance of a very great trade by the multitude of boats and coal keels upon it.' Of the keels, Clerk observed: 'Coal keels are certain sorts of boats that [carry] the coals down to the place where they are embarked [i.e., the coal was loaded on to waiting ships] and generally of an oval form and very thick in the plank because of the Shocks they get in passing the bridge and upon the sides of ships.'

Normally large vessels—ships of 300 tons or more—lay at the mouth of the Tyne but sometimes they made their way upstream to Newcastle as far as the medieval bridge that spanned the river, linking it with Gateshead. Clerk was impressed by the bridge—which was over 700ft (213.3m) long and had a number of houses and shops located upon it—and describes it as magnificent and 'not much inferior to the bridge of London.' Sadly, the structure no longer exists for it was severely damaged by a flood in

84

Opposite: The medieval bridge leading to Newcastle

November 1771 (the only bridge on the river to survive the torrent was at Corbridge) and had to be replaced.

Newcastle's imposing medieval town walls also engaged Clerk's keen attention. They were over two miles (3.2km) long and possessed a number of substantial gateways and towers along their circuit. Of one of the gateways, the Pandon Gate located in the southeast quarter of the town, Clerk concluded that, at least in part, it was 'manifestly Roman' and had no doubt originally served as a gate in Hadrian's Wall built in the second century AD. On this point, the late Professor Eric Birley commented: 'There seems to be no justification for the belief, which Sir John Clerk shared with many other visitors to Newcastle, that the Pandon Gate was Roman; but it may well be that it contained a higher proportion of stones from the Wall than the rest of the town's fortifications.' Of the entranceway, Clerk also wrote: 'This venerable... [gate] is a singular Curiosity though the people of the town seem to have but little regard for it.'

On the day after his arrival in Newcastle, Clerk was visited by a 'very worthy Merchant', namely Charles Atkinson, who proceeded to take him on a sightseeing expedition that included travelling down the river by boat. Of the sights he saw en route, Clerk recorded:

> The sides of the River were cultivated with great care and built for the most part with hewn stone as if every place was designed for a station for ships. The prospect was every way most agreeable for by the multitude of boats and ships the River seemed every where to be in motion. The banks in some places rise very high and are covered with wood and all most the half of what appears seems to be one continued village.

One of the communities in question was North Shields. It had begun life

in the 13th century as a medieval fishing settlement (the fishermen's huts were known as 'shiels'), but its importance as a fishing port had waned. Instead, industrial activity, such as saltmaking, was now a prominent component of the town's economy. Clerk was not impressed by what he saw and thus observed: 'The Shields is a smokey disagreeable place by reason of the multitude of salt pans.' The salt was produced by heating brine in iron pans, using cheap local coal unfit for export.

Having given Shields the thumbs down, Clerk promptly moved on to Tynemouth and walked up to the ruins of Tynemouth Castle, of which he wrote: 'This castle has been strong in old times but now it is entirely neglected.' The castle's defences, of which sections still survive, enclosed a commanding headland and the centrepiece was an imposing gatehouse that still gives access to the site. The gatehouse dates from the late 14th century and was built by the monks of Tynemouth Priory (who were responsible for the defences) and was partly funded by Richard II, who gave £500 towards the costs, and prominent noblemen such as Henry Percy, Earl of Northumberland.

Enclosed within the defences, Clerk found the remains of Tynemouth Priory, which had been the wealthiest monastic house in Northumberland—it was established in the closing years of the 11th century and shut down by Henry VIII in 1539. Of the ruins of the priory, Sir John observed: 'There is here the remains of a Magnificent church and Abbey. Both are well worth the seeing and observing. The church is a piece of excellent Gothic Architecture. Little of the monastery remains.' Fortunately, substantial parts of the church still exist, especially its imposing east end, erected

Tynemouth Priory viewed from the west

about 1200, that rises to a height of 73ft (22.2m) and which served as an important landmark for sailors.

En route back to Newcastle, Clerk visited two glassworks and three collieries. Coalmining had occurred on Tyneside since at least the 13th century, but the local glassmaking industry was of more recent origin. It dated from the early 17th century—by which time wood supplies in traditional centres of glass manufacture such as Surrey were greatly depleted—when a group of gentlemen glassmakers had decided to use coal as an alternative source of furnace fuel and thus set up works on Tyneside. Clerk was particularly struck by the arduous working conditions of the employees; the 'soar labour of the workmen' who looked 'incessantly among the furnaces so that one would wonder how nature can hold out with them.'

Subsequently, Sir John Clerk's exploration of the region included a visit to Hadrian's Wall which fascinated this intelligent, cultured and inquisitive visitor. He carefully studied aspects of the defences and provided his account of his visit with a detailed commentary, complete with diagrams and sketches.

He then left the county by continuing westward into Cumbria.

Opposite: The gatehouse of Tynemouth Castle

WARLIKE AND COLOURFUL BARONS,
THE STORY OF THE UMFRAVILLES

Among families that feature in the history of Northumberland, few rank more prominently than the Umfravilles who were some of the most influential figures in the region for several hundred years.

The family probably came from Offranville near Dieppe in Normandy and a charter states that Robert 'with the beard' (the first member of the line associated with Northumberland) was granted the lordship of Redesdale by William the Conqueror (1066-87). The charter is however generally regarded as a later forgery.

What is certain is that during the reign of Henry I (1100-35) the barony of Prudhoe was granted to a Robert de Umfraville—possibly Robert 'with the beard', or the supposed Robert de Umfraville II. In either case, Umfraville may well have also acquired Redesdale from the same monarch.

The lordships differed significantly. The barony of Prudhoe lay in a fertile stretch of the valley of the Tyne whereas Redesdale was a wilder, more barren place, with poorer soils and a harsher climate. Moreover, whereas Prudhoe lay within Northumberland—and was thus subject to the Sheriff of Northumberland and his officers—Redesdale was a liberty. In other words, with royal permission, it was an area where officers of the Crown were normally excluded and was administered by the Umfravilles and their subordinates. The liberty was approximately 150,000 acres in extent and, in addition to Redesdale, also included adjacent territory. For instance, its northern boundary was formed by the upper reaches of the River Coquet.

During the reign of Henry I, Robert de Umfraville founded a nunnery at Holystone in the valley of the River Coquet. Nunneries were usually not well endowed, and Holystone (whose community numbered 27 nuns in 1313) was likewise not a wealthy house.

Robert possessed a castle at Prudhoe, and was almost certainly responsible for founding a motte and bailey stronghold at Elsdon in Redesdale, a castle erected on high ground on the northeast edge of the village and whose impressive earthworks still survive.

Robert de Umfraville I (or II) died in around 1145, and it was probably little more than a decade later that Elsdon Castle was replaced as the Umfraville fortress in the lordship of Redesdale. Likely in, or shortly after 1157, Henry II ordered the head of the family, Odinel I, to build Harbottle Castle and henceforth this stronghold on high ground overlooking the Coquet served as the capital of the liberty and Elsdon was allowed to decay.

In 1173 King William the Lion of Scotland invaded the North East and expected to receive support from the head of the Umfraville family,

Opposite: Prudhoe Castle

Odinel II, who had been brought up in the household of William's father, who had held the earldom of Northumberland. However, Umfraville refused to comply. Hence William attempted to capture Prudhoe Castle and, according to a contemporary chronicler named Jordan Fantosme, declared of Odinel: 'my father, held him dear and brought him up, but before the end of the day he will regret setting his eyes on me.'

However, William failed to capture Prudhoe. But the following year he invaded again and, after seizing Harbottle Castle, turned his attention on Prudhoe once more. Fantosme tells us that on this occasion William found that Prudhoe had been 'newly provisioned…Odinel had settled some excellent men in the castle, making it such a fortress that I never saw better ones anywhere.'

In the event, the siege only lasted three days during which some damage was done to the defences. Then, having devastated the surrounding country-side, the Scots headed off in the direction of Alnwick, burning and harrying as they did so. Odinel had abandoned Prudhoe as the Scots approached to commence the siege, and was part of an army that now dashed north from Newcastle and captured the Scottish king as he was besieging Alnwick Castle.

Umfraville's extensive possessions (he also held estates in Yorkshire and elsewhere) included high moorland at Kidland in upper Coquetdale, and in 1181 he granted a lease to the Cistercian monks of Newminster Abbey, near Morpeth, so that they could graze sheep at Kidland, moorland approximately 25 miles from their monastery. Odinel retained the right to hunt on the leased land. In addition, he insisted that dogs belonging to the monks were mutilated so that they could not chase game there.

Odinel died in 1182 and in the early 13th century one of his successors, a son named Richard (who became head of the family before Michaelmas 1195) ranked among the opponents of King John and participated in the events that led to Magna Carta and the ensuing civil war. During that conflict only two of Northumberland's barons—Hugh de Balliol of Bywell and Hugh de Bolbec of Styford—sided with the tyrannical king, who came north at the head of an army and, at the beginning of 1216, seized various castles, including Prudhoe which was granted to Balliol. King John soon died, however, and Umfraville regained his lost property in the early days of Henry III.

In 1220 Philip de Oldcoates, the Sheriff of Northumberland, accused Richard, with whom he was at loggerheads, of disregarding a royal prohibition by strengthening Harbottle. Thus the government ordered Umfraville to dismantle the castle, a command to which he and his friends reacted with great indignation. Umfraville successfully argued that the stronghold was 'to the great benefit of the kingdom.'

Richard's son and successor married a Scottish heiress, and the marriage produced a son, Gilbert II, who duly inherited the title Earl of Angus and vast estates in Scotland.

In Northumberland, Gilbert made his presence felt in various ways. In the summer of 1267, for example, the young lord sent a hundred men, some of whom were outlaws from Redesdale, to eject a man named

The scant remains of Harbottle Castle

William Douglas from the manor of Fawdon. This led to the murder of one of Douglas' sons, the theft of money, jewellery and weapons, and the subsequent incarceration of Douglas and another son at Harbottle. As the historian Ralph Robson comments, many records 'show this de Umfraville to have extorted money by menaces, and taken from robbers hush money of up to 100 marks at a time', a substantial sum.

Unlike some other Northumbrians with cross-border links, when Anglo-Scottish conflict erupted in 1296 Gilbert sided with Edward I of England—in that year Harbottle Castle withstood a Scottish assault—and fought north of the border in 1296 and 1298. He died in 1307 and was buried in the church of Hexham Priory (now known as Hexham Abbey) where his effigy can still be seen.

His son and successor Robert de Umfraville also fought in the Scottish wars. Indeed, he participated in the campaign that ended in disaster at Bannockburn in June 1314 and was either captured in the battle or soon taken while in flight. He was ransomed the following year. The aftermath of Bannockburn was a turbulent period for Northumberland, and in 1318 Robert the Bruce of Scotland captured and partly dismantled Harbottle Castle.

Robert de Umfraville died in 1325 and was buried at Newminster Abbey. In the early 1330s his son, Gilbert III, was one of the 'Disinherited' who campaigned in Scotland with the forlorn hope of permanently regaining property and titles that had been lost there during the Wars of Scottish Independence. Moreover, in 1335/6 Gilbert informed the government that Harbottle Castle had been so damaged in 1318 that it could not serve as a suitable prison for the wrongdoers of Redesdale. He thus received royal permission to incarcerate criminals from the liberty at Prudhoe instead. Harbottle was still in ruins in 1351.

The effigy of Gilbert de Umfraville in Hexham Abbey

Gilbert died without surviving issue in 1381, and under an arrangement agreed some years earlier, Prudhoe passed into the hands of Henry Percy, the first Earl of Northumberland, who soon married Gilbert's widow. On the other hand, Gilbert left the liberty of Redesdale to a half-brother named Thomas, and this remained in Umfraville hands until the line became extinct on 27 January 1437 upon the death of a renowned soldier named Robert. It was truly the end of an era.

WHITBURN,
A JEWEL IN SOUTH TYNESIDE

Whitburn lies on the coast between Sunderland and South Shields and is described by John Murray, in a travel guide published in 1864, as 'a pleasant village, on rising ground, with a good view of the sea-coast to the South…. The place is much resorted to in summer for sea-air and bathing, and several houses are let as lodgings.'

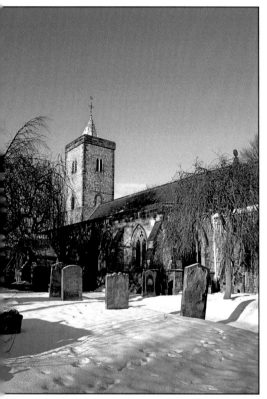

Whitburn Parish Church

Whitburn, whose name is perhaps derived from 'Hwita's barn', is first mentioned in *Boldon Book*, a survey drawn up in the early 1180s on behalf of the landlord, the Bishop of Durham. This tells us that the population included peasants known as villeins and cottagers—the latter held less land—who owed various services and dues to the bishop, such as working on his demesne (located among the village fields) for specified periods. A more exalted peasant, 'John of Whitburn' held a larger holding of 40 acres and one of his obligations was to go on missions for the bishop when required.

Dominating the humble homes of the peasants was Whitburn Parish Church, whose worshippers included residents of the village of Cleadon, a mile or so to the northwest. The church's earliest masonry is apparently Anglo-Saxon and other fabric is medieval. For example, in the 14th or 15th century the upper stage of the tower and the spire were built. Moreover, parts of the church date from a Victorian programme of restoration.

In September 1537 the curate, Robert Hodge, was executed for making treasonable comments about Henry VIII, and two other villagers shared the same fate. Subsequently during the Civil War era, the Parliamentarians ejected the rector, Thomas Triplet, from the living for his Royalist sentiments.

Opposite: The south side of Front Street and part of the village green in 1893.

Just to the east of the church, lies a substantial three-storey Georgian building that was built as the rectory by the Reverend Thomas Baker in 1816. It served that role until the 1930s and is now divided into six exclusive apartments.

In the mid 19th century there were about 115 houses in Whitburn. During this period, the author Lewis Carroll often stayed in the village at the homes of relatives—the earliest record of his doing so is from 1855. Here, he partly occupied his time by sketching the coast. It is claimed, moreover, that he wrote the *Walrus and the Carpenter* in Whitburn. His link with the village is commemorated by a small statue in Whitburn Library.

During his visits, Carroll came into contact with the Williamson family of Whitburn Hall. The Williamsons acquired the hall, which dated from the Elizabethan era and lay to the east of the rectory, in 1719 and last lived there in the mid 20th century. Horse racing ranked high among the interests of the sixth baronet, Sir Hedworth Williamson, and he owned a number of racehorses, including winners of the Derby in 1803 and 1808, that were trained on Whitburn beach. The eighth baronet, also named Hedworth, was likewise interested in sport and in 1862 he became the first president of Whitburn Cricket Club, to whom he granted permission to play matches on ground in front of his home. Indeed, he took to the pitch himself and was evidently a competent all rounder. Although the cricket club still exists, sadly the hall was demolished in 1980.

The attractive village green lies little more than a stone's throw to the north of the church, and is overlooked by some fine houses. The most prominent is Whitburn House, a mock-Tudor structure with features reminiscent of buildings in the Alps. It was built in 1869 for Thomas Barnes, a local bigwig, and has been described by the architectural historian Sir Nikolaus Pevsner as an 'extravaganza'.

The green lies beside a road running eastward to link up with the coastal road. When heading northward along the latter, one sees Whitburn Mill,

The eye-catching Whitburn House

which is mostly built of magnesian limestone quarried locally. It dates from the 1790s and replaced a wooden structure blown down in a storm. The mill, lovingly restored in recent years, ceased to work in the late 1870s. Nevertheless it remained useful for the *Sunderland Daily Post* noted on 31 July 1880:

'This old familiar Sea Mark or Land Mark, is not going to be lost to the pilots and fishermen. Mr. Thomas Barnes of Whitburn, on whose land the mill stands, has reroofed it, walled up windows to the North and East, taken out the mill gear and turned the lower storey into a harbour for his Herefords, with hay & straw chamber above.'

The mill, which is occasionally opened to the public, lies amid housing constructed in the second half of the 20th century—a century in which Whitburn expanded considerably—and is an appealing link with Whitburn's long past.

Whitburn Mill

SELECT BIBLIOGRAPHY

Birley, E., 'Sir John Clerk's Visit to the North of England in 1724', *Transactions of the Architectural and Archaeological Society of Durham and Northumberland*, vol. XI, 1962

Colls, R., (ed.), *Northumbria – History and Identity 547-2000*, 2007

Cunningham, H., *Grace Darling—Victorian Heroine*, 2007

Dodds, G.L., *Historic Sites of Northumberland and Newcastle upon Tyne*, (revised edition), 2002

Faulkner, T.E., *Northumbrian Panorama: Studies in the History and Culture of North East England*, 1996

Fraser, C. & Emsley, K., *Northumbria*, 1989

Guy, A., *Steam and Speed – Railways of Tyne & Wear from the Earliest Days*, 2003

Hepple, L.W., *A History of Northumberland and Newcastle upon Tyne*, 1976

Linsley, S., *Ports and Harbours of Northumberland*, 2005

Lomas, R., *An Encyclopaedia of North-East England*, 2009

Manders, F., *Cinemas of Newcastle*, (revised edition), 2005

Purdue, A.W., *Newcastle: the Biography*, 2011

Robson, R., *The Rise and Fall of the English Highland Clans*, 1989

Saint, A., *Cragside*, 1992

Southey, R., Maddison, M., & Hughes, D., *The Ingenious Mr Avison: Making Music and Money in Eighteenth-Century Newcastle*, 2009

PICTURE CREDITS

ALSO BY GLEN LYNDON DODDS:

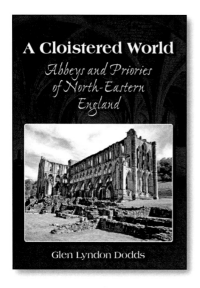

A Cloistered World – Abbeys and Priories of North-Eastern England, (hardback, £12.99)

North-eastern England has much to offer anyone interested in exploring medieval abbeys and priories, and this beautifully illustrated book, primarily written for the general public, provides a readable and informative introduction to the subject.

A stimulating introductory chapter is followed by a discussion of the history and standing remains of over 20 former religious houses, including Brinkburn Priory, Durham Cathedral Priory, Hexham Abbey, Lindisfarne Priory and Tynemouth Priory. The lively and reliable text is accompanied by 58 colour photographs.

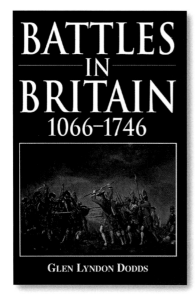

Forthcoming on Amazon Kindle:

Battles in Britain 1066-1746

First published by Arms & Armour Press in 1996, this well researched book (which received favourable comment from Bryan Perrett and the late Professor Richard Holmes) contains detailed accounts of nine significant battles, including Hastings, Flodden, Marston Moor and Culloden, and also has shorter chapters on 19 other engagements, including Halidon Hill and Otterburn.